Travel phrasebooks collection
«Everything Will Be ...

# PHRASEBOOK

## — POLISH —

# THE MOST IMPORTANT PHRASES

This phrasebook contains
the most important
phrases and questions
for basic communication
Everything you need
to survive overseas

By Andrey Taranov

**T&P BOOKS**

## Phrasebook + 1500-word dictionary

# English-Polish phrasebook & concise dictionary

By Andrey Taranov

The collection of "Everything Will Be Okay" travel phrasebooks published by T&P Books is designed for people traveling abroad for tourism and business. The phrasebooks contain what matters most - the essentials for basic communication. This is an indispensable set of phrases to "survive" while abroad.

Another section of the book also provides a small dictionary with more than 1,500 useful words arranged alphabetically. The dictionary includes a lot of gastronomic terms and will be helpful when ordering food at a restaurant or buying groceries at the store.

T&P Books Publishing
www.tpbooks.com

ISBN: 978-1-78492-443-0

This book is also available in E-book formats.
Please visit www.tpbooks.com or the major online bookstores.

# FOREWORD

The collection of "Everything Will Be Okay" travel phrasebooks published by T&P Books is designed for people traveling abroad for tourism and business. The phrasebooks contain what matters most - the essentials for basic communication. This is an indispensable set of phrases to "survive" while abroad.

This phrasebook will help you in most cases where you need to ask something, get directions, find out how much something costs, etc. It can also resolve difficult communication situations where gestures just won't help.

This book contains a lot of phrases that have been grouped according to the most relevant topics. A separate section of the book also provides a small dictionary with more than 1,500 important and useful words.

Take "Everything Will Be Okay" phrasebook with you on the road and you'll have an irreplaceable traveling companion who will help you find your way out of any situation and teach you to not fear speaking with foreigners.

# TABLE OF CONTENTS

T&P Books Publishing

# PRONUNCIATION

| Letter | Polish example | T&P phonetic alphabet | English example |
|--------|----------------|-----------------------|-----------------|

## Vowels

| Letter | Polish example | T&P phonetic alphabet | English example |
|--------|----------------|-----------------------|-----------------|
| A a | fala | [a] | shorter than in ask |
| Ą ą | są | [ɔ̃] | strong |
| E e | tekst | [ɛ] | man, bad |
| Ę ę | pięć | [ɛ] | fang |
| I i | niski | [i] | shorter than in feet |
| O o | strona | [ɔ] | bottle, doctor |
| Ó ó | ołów | [u] | book |
| U u | ulica | [u] | book |
| Y y | stalowy | [ɪ] | big, America |

## Consonants

| Letter | Polish example | T&P phonetic alphabet | English example |
|--------|----------------|-----------------------|-----------------|
| B b | brew | [b] | baby, book |
| C c | palec | [ts] | cats, tsetse fly |
| Ć ć | haftować | [tʃ] | church, French |
| D d | modny | [d] | day, doctor |
| F f | perfumy | [f] | face, food |
| G g | zegarek | [g] | game, gold |
| H h | handel | [h] | huge, hat |
| J j | jajko | [j] | yes, New York |
| K k | krab | [k] | clock, kiss |
| L l | mleko | [l] | lace, people |
| Ł ł | głodny | [w] | vase, winter |
| M m | guma | [m] | magic, milk |
| N n | Indie | [n] | name, normal |
| Ń ń | jesień | [ɲ] | canyon, new |
| P p | poczta | [p] | pencil, private |
| R r | portret | [r] | rice, radio |
| S s | studnia | [s] | city, boss |
| Ś ś | świat | [ɕ] | sheep, shop |

| Letter | Polish example | T&P phonetic alphabet | English example |
|--------|----------------|----------------------|-----------------|
| T t | taniec | [t] | tune, student |
| W w | wieczór | [v] | very, river |
| Z z | zachód | [z] | zebra, please |
| Ź ź | żaba | [ʑ] | gigolo |
| Ż ż | żagiel | [ʒ] | forge, pleasure |

## Combinations of letters

| ch | ich, zachód | [h] | huge, humor |
|----|-------------|-----|-------------|
| ci | kwiecień | [tɕ] | cheese |
| cz | czasami | [tʃ] | church, French |
| dz | dzbanek | [dz] | beads, kids |
| dzi | dziecko | [dʑ] | jeans, gene |
| dź | dźwig | [dʑ] | jeans, gene |
| dż | dżinsy | [j] | yes, New York |
| ni | niedziela | [ɲ] | canyon, new |
| rz | orzech | [ʒ] | forge, pleasure |
| si | osiem | [ɕ] | sheep, shop |
| sz | paszport | [ʃ] | machine, shark |
| zi | zima | [ʑ] | gigolo |

## Comments

' Letters Qq, Vv, Xx used in foreign loanwords only

# LIST OF ABBREVIATIONS

## English abbreviations

| | | |
|---|---|---|
| ab. | - | about |
| adj | - | adjective |
| adv | - | adverb |
| anim. | - | animate |
| as adj | - | attributive noun used as adjective |
| e.g. | - | for example |
| etc. | - | et cetera |
| fam. | - | familiar |
| fem. | - | feminine |
| form. | - | formal |
| inanim. | - | inanimate |
| masc. | - | masculine |
| math | - | mathematics |
| mil. | - | military |
| n | - | noun |
| pl | - | plural |
| pron. | - | pronoun |
| sb | - | somebody |
| sing. | - | singular |
| sth | - | something |
| v aux | - | auxiliary verb |
| vi | - | intransitive verb |
| vi, vt | - | intransitive, transitive verb |
| vt | - | transitive verb |

## Polish abbreviations

| | | |
|---|---|---|
| ż | - | feminine noun |
| ż, l.mn. | - | feminine plural |
| l.mn. | - | plural |
| m | - | masculine noun |
| m, ż | - | masculine, feminine |
| m, l.mn. | - | masculine plural |
| n | - | neuter |

# POLISH
# PHRASEBOOK

This section contains important phrases that may come in handy in various real-life situations.
The phrasebook will help you ask for directions, clarify a price, buy tickets, and order food at a restaurant

**T&P Books Publishing**

# PHRASEBOOK
# CONTENTS

T&P Books Publishing

# The bare minimum

| | |
|---|---|
| Excuse me, ... | **Przepraszam, ...**<br>[pʃɛ'praʃam, ...] |
| Hello. | **Witam.**<br>['vʲitam] |
| Thank you. | **Dziękuję.**<br>[dʑiɛŋ'kujɛ] |
| Good bye. | **Do widzenia.**<br>[dɔ vʲi'dzɛɲa] |
| Yes. | **Tak.**<br>[tak] |
| No. | **Nie.**<br>[ɲɛ] |
| I don't know. | **Nie wiem.**<br>[ɲɛ 'vʲɛm] |
| Where? \| Where to? \| When? | **Gdzie? \| Dokąd? \| Kiedy?**<br>[gdʑɛ? \| 'dɔkɔnt? \| 'kʲɛdi?] |

| | |
|---|---|
| I need ... | **Potrzebuję ...**<br>[pɔtʃɛ'bujɛ ...] |
| I want ... | **Chcę ...**<br>['xtsɛ ...] |
| Do you have ...? | **Czy jest ...?**<br>[tʃɨ 'jɛst ...?] |
| Is there a ... here? | **Czy jest tutaj ...?**<br>[tʃɨ 'jɛst 'tutaj ...?] |
| May I ...? | **Czy mogę ...?**<br>[tʃɨ 'mɔgɛ ...?] |
| ..., please (polite request) | **..., poproszę**<br>[..., pɔ'prɔʃɛ] |

| | |
|---|---|
| I'm looking for ... | **Szukam ...**<br>['ʃukam ...] |
| restroom | **toalety**<br>[tɔa'lɛti] |
| ATM | **bankomatu**<br>[bankɔ'matu] |
| pharmacy (drugstore) | **apteki**<br>[a'ptɛkʲi] |
| hospital | **szpitala**<br>[ʃpʲi'tala] |
| police station | **komendy policji**<br>[kɔ'mɛndɨ pɔ'ʎitsji] |
| subway | **metra**<br>['mɛtra] |

| | |
|---|---|
| taxi | **taksówki**<br>[ta'ksufkʲi] |
| train station | **dworca kolejowego**<br>['dvɔrtsa kɔlɛjɔ'vɛgɔ] |

| | |
|---|---|
| My name is … | **Mam na imię …**<br>[mam na 'imʲiɛ …] |
| What's your name? | **Jak pan /pani/ ma na imię?**<br>['jak pan /'paɲi/ ma na 'imʲiɛ?] |
| Could you please help me? | **Czy może pan /pani/ mi pomóc?**<br>[tʃɨ 'mɔʒɛ pan /'paɲi/ mʲi 'pɔmuts?] |
| I've got a problem. | **Mam problem.**<br>[mam 'prɔblɛm] |
| I don't feel well. | **Źle się czuję.**<br>[zlɛ ɕiɛ 'tʃujɛ] |
| Call an ambulance! | **Proszę wezwać karetkę!**<br>['prɔʃɛ 'vɛzvatɕ ka'rɛtkɛ!] |
| May I make a call? | **Czy mogę zadzwonić?**<br>[tʃɨ 'mɔgɛ za'dzvɔɲitɕ?] |

| | |
|---|---|
| I'm sorry. | **Przepraszam.**<br>[pʃɛ'praʃam] |
| You're welcome. | **Proszę bardzo.**<br>['prɔʃɛ 'bardzɔ] |

| | |
|---|---|
| I, me | **ja**<br>['ja] |
| you (inform.) | **ty**<br>['tɨ] |
| he | **on**<br>[ɔn] |
| she | **ona**<br>['ɔna] |
| they (masc.) | **oni**<br>['ɔɲi] |
| they (fem.) | **one**<br>['ɔnɛ] |
| we | **my**<br>['mɨ] |
| you (pl) | **wy**<br>['vɨ] |
| you (sg, form.) | **pan /pani/**<br>[pan /'paɲi/] |

| | |
|---|---|
| ENTRANCE | **WEJŚCIE**<br>['vɛjɕtɕɛ] |
| EXIT | **WYJŚCIE**<br>['vɨjɕtɕɛ] |
| OUT OF ORDER | **NIECZYNNY**<br>[ɲɛ'tʃɨnnɨ] |
| CLOSED | **ZAMKNIĘTE**<br>[za'mkɲiɛntɛ] |

| OPEN | **OTWARTE** |
| | [ɔ'tfartɛ] |
| FOR WOMEN | **PANIE** |
| | ['paɲɛ] |
| FOR MEN | **PANOWIE** |
| | [pa'nɔvʲɛ] |

## Questions

| | |
|---|---|
| Where? | **Gdzie?**<br>[gdzɛ?] |
| Where to? | **Dokąd?**<br>['dɔkɔnt?] |
| Where from? | **Skąd?**<br>['skɔnt?] |
| Why? | **Dlaczego?**<br>[dla'ʧɛgɔ?] |
| For what reason? | **Dlaczego?**<br>[dla'ʧɛgɔ?] |
| When? | **Kiedy?**<br>['kʲɛdi?] |
| How long? | **Jak długo?**<br>['jag 'dwugɔ?] |
| At what time? | **O której godzinie?**<br>[ɔ 'kturɛj gɔ'dʑiɲɛ?] |
| How much? | **Ile kosztuje?**<br>['ilɛ kɔ'ʃtujɛ?] |
| Do you have ...? | **Czy jest ...?**<br>[ʧi 'jɛst ...?] |
| Where is ...? | **Gdzie jest ...?**<br>[gdʑɛ 'jɛst ...?] |
| What time is it? | **Która godzina?**<br>['ktura gɔ'dʑina?] |
| May I make a call? | **Czy mogę zadzwonić?**<br>[ʧi 'mɔgɛ za'dzvɔɲitɕ?] |
| Who's there? | **Kto tam?**<br>[ktɔ tam?] |
| Can I smoke here? | **Czy mogę tu zapalić?**<br>[ʧi 'mɔgɛ tu za'paʎitɕ?] |
| May I ...? | **Czy mogę ...?**<br>[ʧi 'mɔgɛ ...?] |

# Needs

| I'd like ... | Chciałbym /Chciałabym/ ...<br>['xtɕawbɨm /xtɕa'wabɨm/ ...] |
| I don't want ... | Nie chcę ...<br>[ɲɛ 'xtsɛ ...] |
| I'm thirsty. | Jestem spragniony /spragniona/.<br>['jɛstɛm spra'gɲoni /spra'gɲona/] |
| I want to sleep. | Chce mi się spać.<br>['xtsɛ mʲi ɕɛ 'spatɕ] |

| I want ... | Chcę ...<br>['xtsɛ ...] |
| to wash up | umyć się<br>['umɨtɕ ɕɛ] |
| to brush my teeth | umyć zęby<br>['umɨtɕ 'zɛmbɨ] |
| to rest a while | trochę odpocząć<br>['trɔxɛ ɔ'tpɔtʃɔntɕ] |
| to change my clothes | zmienić ubranie<br>['zmʲɛɲitɕ u'braɲɛ] |

| to go back to the hotel | wrócić do hotelu<br>['vrutɕitɕ dɔ xɔ'tɛlu] |
| to buy ... | kupić ...<br>['kupʲitɕ ...] |
| to go to ... | iść ...<br>['iɕtɕ ...] |
| to visit ... | odwiedzić ...<br>[ɔ'dvʲɛdzitɕ ...] |
| to meet with ... | spotkać się z ...<br>['spɔtkatɕ ɕɛ s ...] |
| to make a call | zadzwonić<br>[za'dzvɔɲitɕ] |

| I'm tired. | Jestem zmęczony /zmęczona/.<br>['jɛstɛm zmɛ'ntʃɔnɨ /zmɛ'ntʃɔna/] |
| We are tired. | Jesteśmy zmęczeni /zmęczone/.<br>[jɛs'tɛɕmɨ zmɛ'ntʃɛɲi /zmɛ'ntʃɔnɛ/] |
| I'm cold. | Jest mi zimno.<br>['jɛst mʲi 'zimnɔ] |
| I'm hot. | Jest mi gorąco.<br>['jɛst mʲi gɔ'rɔntsɔ] |
| I'm OK. | W porządku.<br>[f pɔ'ʒɔntku] |

I need to make a call.

**Muszę zadzwonić.**
['muʃɛ za'dzvɔɲiʨ]

I need to go to the restroom.

**Muszę iść do toalety.**
['muʃɛ 'iɕʨ dɔ tɔa'lɛti]

I have to go.

**Muszę iść.**
['muʃɛ 'iɕʨ]

I have to go now.

**Muszę już iść.**
['muʃɛ 'juʒ 'iɕʨ]

## Asking for directions

| | |
|---|---|
| Excuse me, ... | **Przepraszam, ...** <br> [pʃɛ'praʃam, ...] |
| Where is ...? | **Gdzie jest ...?** <br> [gdʑɛ 'jɛst ...?] |
| Which way is ...? | **W którą stronę jest ...?** <br> [f 'kturɔ̃ 'strɔnɛ 'jɛst ...?] |
| Could you help me, please? | **Czy może pan /pani/ mi pomóc?** <br> [tʃɨ 'mɔʒɛ pan /'paɲi/ mʲi 'pɔmuts?] |

| | |
|---|---|
| I'm looking for ... | **Szukam ...** <br> ['ʃukam ...] |
| I'm looking for the exit. | **Szukam wyjścia.** <br> ['ʃukam 'vɨjɕtɕa] |
| I'm going to ... | **Jadę do ...** <br> ['jadɛ dɔ ...] |
| Am I going the right way to ...? | **Czy idę w dobrym kierunku do ...?** <br> [tʃɨ 'idɛ v 'dɔbrɨm kʲɛ'runku 'dɔ ...?] |

| | |
|---|---|
| Is it far? | **Czy to daleko?** <br> [tʃɨ tɔ da'lɛkɔ?] |
| Can I get there on foot? | **Czy mogę tam dojść pieszo?** <br> [tʃɨ 'mɔgɛ tam 'dɔjɕtɕ 'pʲɛʃɔ?] |
| Can you show me on the map? | **Czy może mi pan /pani/ pokazać na mapie?** <br> [tʃɨ 'mɔʒɛ mʲi pan /'paɲi/ pɔ'kazatɕ na 'mapʲɛ?] |
| Show me where we are right now. | **Proszę mi pokazać gdzie teraz jesteśmy.** <br> ['prɔʃɛ mʲi pɔ'kazatɕ gdʑɛ 'tɛras jɛ'stɛɕmɨ] |

| | |
|---|---|
| Here | **Tutaj** <br> ['tutaj] |
| There | **Tam** <br> [tam] |
| This way | **Tędy** <br> ['tɛndɨ] |

| | |
|---|---|
| Turn right. | **Należy skręcić w prawo.** <br> [na'lɛʒɨ 'skrɛntɕitɕ f 'pravɔ] |
| Turn left. | **Należy skręcić w lewo.** <br> [na'lɛʒɨ 'skrɛntɕitɕ v 'lɛvɔ] |
| first (second, third) turn | **pierwszy (drugi, trzeci) skręt** <br> ['pʲɛrfʃɨ ('drugi, 'tʃɛtɕi) 'skrɛnt] |

to the right          **w prawo**
[f 'pravɔ]

to the left           **w lewo**
[v 'lɛvɔ]

Go straight.         **Proszę iść prosto.**
['prɔʃɛ 'iɕtɕ 'prɔstɔ]

# Signs

| | |
|---|---|
| WELCOME! | **WITAMY!**<br>[vʲi'tamɨ!] |
| ENTRANCE | **WEJŚCIE**<br>['vɛjɕtɕɛ] |
| EXIT | **WYJŚCIE**<br>['vɨjɕtɕɛ] |

| | |
|---|---|
| PUSH | **PCHAĆ**<br>['pxatɕ] |
| PULL | **CIĄGNĄĆ**<br>['tɕiɔŋgnɔntɕ] |
| OPEN | **OTWARTE**<br>[ɔ'tfartɛ] |
| CLOSED | **ZAMKNIĘTE**<br>[za'mkɲiɛntɛ] |

| | |
|---|---|
| FOR WOMEN | **PANIE**<br>['paɲɛ] |
| FOR MEN | **PANOWIE**<br>[pa'nɔvʲɛ] |
| MEN, GENTS | **TOALETA MĘSKA**<br>[tɔa'lɛta 'mɛ̃ska] |
| WOMEN, LADIES | **TOALETA DAMSKA**<br>[tɔa'lɛta 'damska] |

| | |
|---|---|
| DISCOUNTS | **ZNIŻKI**<br>['zɲiʃkʲi] |
| SALE | **WYPRZEDAŻ**<br>[vɨ'pʃɛdaʒ] |
| FREE | **ZA DARMO**<br>[za 'darmɔ] |
| NEW! | **NOWOŚĆ!**<br>['nɔvɔɕtɕ!] |
| ATTENTION! | **UWAGA!**<br>[u'vaga!] |

| | |
|---|---|
| NO VACANCIES | **BRAK WOLNYCH MIEJSC**<br>['brag 'vɔlnix 'mʲɛjsts] |
| RESERVED | **REZERWACJA**<br>[rɛzɛ'rvatsja] |
| ADMINISTRATION | **ADMINISTRACJA**<br>[admʲiɲi'stratsja] |
| STAFF ONLY | **TYLKO DLA PERSONELU**<br>['tɨlkɔ 'dla pɛrsɔ'nɛlu] |

| | |
|---|---|
| BEWARE OF THE DOG! | **UWAGA PIES** [u'vaga 'pʲɛs] |
| NO SMOKING! | **ZAKAZ PALENIA** ['zakas pa'lɛɲa] |
| DO NOT TOUCH! | **NIE DOTYKAĆ!** [ɲɛ do'tikatɕ!] |
| DANGEROUS | **NIEBEZPIECZNE** [ɲɛbɛ'spʲɛtʃnɛ] |
| DANGER | **NIEBEZPIECZEŃSTWO** [ɲɛbɛspʲɛ'tʃɛnstfɔ] |
| HIGH VOLTAGE | **WYSOKIE NAPIĘCIE** [vɨ'sɔkʲɛ na'pʲiɛntɕɛ] |
| NO SWIMMING! | **ZAKAZ PŁYWANIA** ['zakas pwɨ'vaɲa] |
| | |
| OUT OF ORDER | **NIECZYNNY** [ɲɛ'tʃɨnnɨ] |
| FLAMMABLE | **ŁATWOPALNY** [watfɔ'palnɨ] |
| FORBIDDEN | **ZABRONIONE** [zabrɔ'ɲɔnɛ] |
| NO TRESPASSING! | **WSTĘP WZBRONIONY!** ['fstɛmb vzbrɔ'ɲɔnɨ!] |
| WET PAINT | **ŚWIEŻO MALOWANE** ['ɕvʲɛʒɔ malɔ'vanɛ] |
| | |
| CLOSED FOR RENOVATIONS | **ZAMKNIĘTE NA CZAS REMONTU** [za'mkɲiɛntɛ na 'tʃaz rɛ'mɔntu] |
| WORKS AHEAD | **ROBOTY DROGOWE** [rɔ'bɔtɨ drɔ'gɔvɛ] |
| DETOUR | **OBJAZD** ['ɔbjazt] |

## Transportation. General phrases

| | |
|---|---|
| plane | **samolot**<br>[sa'mɔlɔt] |
| train | **pociąg**<br>['pɔtɕiɔŋk] |
| bus | **autobus**<br>[aw'tɔbus] |
| ferry | **prom**<br>['prɔm] |
| taxi | **taksówka**<br>[ta'ksufka] |
| car | **samochód**<br>[sa'mɔxut] |

| | |
|---|---|
| schedule | **rozkład jazdy \| rozkład lotów**<br>['rɔskwat 'jazdɨ \| 'rɔskwat 'lɔtuf] |
| Where can I see the schedule? | **Gdzie znajdę rozkład jazdy?**<br>[gdʑɛ 'znajdɛ 'rɔskwat 'jazdɨ?] |
| workdays (weekdays) | **dni robocze**<br>['dɲi rɔ'bɔtʃɛ] |
| weekends | **weekend**<br>[vɛ'ɛkɛnt] |
| holidays | **święta**<br>['ɕviɛnta] |

| | |
|---|---|
| DEPARTURE | **WYJAZDY \| PRZYLOTY**<br>[vɨ'jazdɨ \| pʃɨ'lɔtɨ] |
| ARRIVAL | **PRZYJAZDY \| ODLOTY**<br>[pʃɨ'jazdɨ \| ɔ'dlɔtɨ] |
| DELAYED | **OPÓŹNIONY**<br>[ɔpu'ʑɲɔnɨ] |
| CANCELED | **ODWOŁANY**<br>[ɔdvɔ'wanɨ] |

| | |
|---|---|
| next (train, etc.) | **następny**<br>[na'stɛmpnɨ] |
| first | **pierwszy**<br>['piɛrfʃɨ] |
| last | **ostatni**<br>[ɔ'statɲi] |

| | |
|---|---|
| When is the next ...? | **O której jest następny ...?**<br>[ɔ 'kturɛj 'jɛst na'stɛmpnɨ ...?] |
| When is the first ...? | **O której jest pierwszy ...?**<br>[ɔ 'kturɛj 'jɛst 'piɛrfʃɨ ...?] |

When is the last ...?

**O której jest ostatni ...?**
[ɔ 'kturɛj 'jɛst ɔ'statɲi ...?]

transfer (change of trains, etc.)

**przesiadka**
[pʃɛ'ɕatka]

to make a transfer

**przesiąść się**
['pʃɛɕiɔ̃ɕtɕ ɕiɛ]

Do I need to make a transfer?

**Czy muszę się przesiadać?**
[tʃɨ 'muʃɛ ɕiɛ pʃɛ'ɕadatɕ?]

# Buying tickets

| | |
|---|---|
| Where can I buy tickets? | **Gdzie mogę kupić bilety?**<br>[gdʑɛ 'mɔgɛ 'kupʲitɕ bʲi'lɛti?] |
| ticket | **bilet**<br>['bʲilɛt] |
| to buy a ticket | **kupić bilet**<br>['kupʲitɕ 'bʲilɛt] |
| ticket price | **cena biletu**<br>['tsɛna bʲi'lɛtu] |

| | |
|---|---|
| Where to? | **Dokąd?**<br>['dɔkɔnt?] |
| To what station? | **Do której stacji?**<br>[dɔ 'kturɛj 'statsji?] |
| I need ... | **Poproszę ...**<br>[pɔ'prɔʃɛ ...] |
| one ticket | **jeden bilet**<br>['jɛdɛn 'bʲilɛt] |
| two tickets | **dwa bilety**<br>['dva bʲi'lɛti] |
| three tickets | **trzy bilety**<br>[tʃɨ bʲi'lɛti] |

| | |
|---|---|
| one-way | **w jedną stronę**<br>[f 'jɛdnɔ̃ 'strɔnɛ] |
| round-trip | **w obie strony**<br>[v 'ɔbʲɛ 'strɔni] |
| first class | **pierwsza klasa**<br>['pʲɛrfʃa 'klasa] |
| second class | **druga klasa**<br>['druga 'klasa] |

| | |
|---|---|
| today | **dzisiaj**<br>['dʑiɕaj] |
| tomorrow | **jutro**<br>['jutrɔ] |
| the day after tomorrow | **pojutrze**<br>[pɔ'jutʃɛ] |
| in the morning | **rano**<br>['ranɔ] |
| in the afternoon | **po południu**<br>[pɔ pɔ'wudɲu] |
| in the evening | **wieczorem**<br>[vʲɛ'tʃɔrɛm] |

aisle seat

**miejsce przy przejściu**
['mʲɛjstsɛ pʃi 'pʃɛjɕtɕu]

window seat

**miejsce przy oknie**
['mʲɛjstsɛ pʃi 'ɔkɲɛ]

How much?

**Ile kosztuje?**
['ilɛ kɔ'ʃtujɛ?]

Can I pay by credit card?

**Czy mogę zapłacić kartą?**
[tʃi 'mɔgɛ za'pwatɕitɕ 'kartɔ̃?]

# Bus

| | |
|---|---|
| bus | **autobus**<br>[aw'tɔbus] |
| intercity bus | **autobus międzymiastowy**<br>[aw'tɔbus mʲiɛndzimʲa'stɔvɨ] |
| bus stop | **przystanek autobusowy**<br>[pʃi'stanɛk awtɔbu'sɔvɨ] |
| Where's the nearest bus stop? | **Gdzie jest najbliższy przystanek autobusowy?**<br>[gdʑɛ 'jɛst najb'ʎiʃʃɨ pʃi'stanɛk awtɔbu'sɔvɨ?] |

| | |
|---|---|
| number (bus ~, etc.) | **numer**<br>['numɛr] |
| Which bus do I take to get to ...? | **Którym autobusem dojadę do ...?**<br>['kturɨm awtɔ'busɛm dɔ'jadɛ dɔ ...?] |
| Does this bus go to ...? | **Czy ten autobus jedzie do ...?**<br>[tʃɨ 'tɛn aw'tɔbus 'jɛdʑɛ dɔ ...?] |
| How frequent are the buses? | **Jak często jeżdżą autobusy?**<br>['jak 'tʃɛ̃stɔ 'jɛʒdʒɔ̃ awtɔ'busɨ?] |

| | |
|---|---|
| every 15 minutes | **co piętnaście minut**<br>['tsɔ pʲiɛ'ntnaɕtɕɛ 'mʲinut] |
| every half hour | **co pół godziny**<br>['tsɔ 'puw gɔ'dʑinɨ] |
| every hour | **co godzinę**<br>['tsɔ gɔ'dʑinɛ] |
| several times a day | **kilka razy dziennie**<br>['kʲilka 'razɨ 'dʑɛnɲɛ] |
| ... times a day | **... razy dziennie**<br>[... 'razɨ 'dʑɛnɲɛ] |

| | |
|---|---|
| schedule | **rozkład jazdy**<br>['rɔskwat 'jazdɨ] |
| Where can I see the schedule? | **Gdzie znajdę rozkład jazdy?**<br>[gdʑɛ 'znajdɛ 'rɔskwat 'jazdɨ?] |

| | |
|---|---|
| When is the next bus? | **O której jest następny autobus?**<br>[ɔ 'kturɛj 'jɛst na'stɛmpnɨ aw'tɔbus?] |
| When is the first bus? | **O której jest pierwszy autobus?**<br>[ɔ 'kturɛj 'jɛst 'pʲɛrfʃɨ aw'tɔbus?] |
| When is the last bus? | **O której jest ostatni autobus?**<br>[ɔ 'kturɛj 'jɛst ɔ'statɲi aw'tɔbus?] |
| stop | **przystanek**<br>[pʃi'stanɛk] |

next stop

**następny przystanek**
[na'stɛmpnɨ pʃɨ'stanɛk]

last stop (terminus)

**ostatni przystanek**
[ɔ'statɲi pʃɨ'stanɛk]

Stop here, please.

**Proszę się tu zatrzymać.**
['prɔʃɛ ɕiɛ tu za'tʃɨmatɕ]

Excuse me, this is my stop.

**Przepraszam, to mój przystanek.**
[pʃɛ'praʃam, tɔ muj pʃɨ'stanɛk]

# Train

| | |
|---|---|
| train | **pociąg**<br>['potɕiɔŋk] |
| suburban train | **kolejka**<br>[kɔ'lɛjka] |
| long-distance train | **pociąg dalekobieżny**<br>['potɕiɔŋk dalɛkɔ'bʲɛʒnɨ] |
| train station | **dworzec kolejowy**<br>['dvɔʒɛts kɔlɛ'jɔvɨ] |
| Excuse me, where is the exit to the platform? | **Przepraszam, gdzie jest wyjście z peronu?**<br>[pʃɛ'praʃam, gdʑɛ 'jɛsd 'vɨjɕtɕɛ s pɛ'rɔnu?] |

| | |
|---|---|
| Does this train go to …? | **Czy ten pociąg jedzie do …?**<br>[tʃɨ 'tɛn 'potɕiɔŋk 'jɛdʑɛ dɔ …?] |
| next train | **następny pociąg**<br>[na'stɛmpnɨ 'potɕiɔŋk] |
| When is the next train? | **O której jest następny pociąg?**<br>[ɔ 'kturɛj 'jɛst na'stɛmpnɨ 'potɕiɔŋk?] |
| Where can I see the schedule? | **Gdzie znajdę rozkład jazdy?**<br>[gdʑɛ 'znajdɛ 'rɔskwat 'jazdɨ?] |
| From which platform? | **Z którego peronu?**<br>[s ktu'rɛgɔ pɛ'rɔnu?] |
| When does the train arrive in …? | **O której ten pociąg dojeżdża do …?**<br>[ɔ 'kturɛj 'tɛn 'potɕiɔŋk dɔ'jɛʒdʒa dɔ …?] |

| | |
|---|---|
| Please help me. | **Proszę mi pomóc.**<br>['prɔʃɛ mʲi 'pomuts] |
| I'm looking for my seat. | **Szukam swojego miejsca.**<br>['ʃukam sfɔ'jɛgɔ 'mʲɛjstsa] |
| We're looking for our seats. | **Szukamy naszych miejsc.**<br>[ʃu'kamɨ 'naʃix 'mʲɛjsts] |
| My seat is taken. | **Moje miejsce jest zajęte.**<br>['mɔjɛ 'mʲɛjstsɛ 'jɛsd za'jɛntɛ] |
| Our seats are taken. | **Nasze miejsca są zajęte.**<br>['naʃɛ 'mʲɛjstsa 'sɔ̃ za'jɛntɛ] |

| | |
|---|---|
| I'm sorry but this is my seat. | **Przykro mi ale to moje miejsce.**<br>['pʃɨkrɔ mʲi 'alɛ tɔ 'mɔjɛ 'mʲɛjstsɛ] |
| Is this seat taken? | **Czy to miejsce jest zajęte?**<br>[tʃɨ tɔ 'mʲɛjstsɛ 'jɛsd za'jɛntɛ?] |
| May I sit here? | **Czy mogę tu usiąść?**<br>[tʃɨ 'mɔgɛ tu 'uɕiɔ̃ɕtɕ?] |

## On the train. Dialogue (No ticket)

Ticket, please.

**Bilety, proszę.**
[bʲi'lɛtɨ, 'prɔʃɛ]

I don't have a ticket.

**Nie mam biletu.**
[ɲɛ 'mam bʲi'lɛtu]

I lost my ticket.

**Zgubiłem bilet.**
[zgu'bʲiwɛm 'bʲilɛt]

I forgot my ticket at home.

**Zostawiłem bilet w domu.**
[zɔsta'vʲiwɛm 'bʲilɛt v 'dɔmu]

You can buy a ticket from me.

**Może pan /pani/ kupić bilet ode mnie.**
['mɔʒɛ pan /'paɲi/ 'kupʲitɕ 'bʲilɛt 'ɔdɛ 'mɲɛ]

You will also have to pay a fine.

**Będzie pan musiał /pani musiała/ również zapłacić mandat.**
['bɛndʑɛ pan 'muɕaw /'paɲi mu'ɕawa/ 'ruvɲɛʒ za'pwatɕitɕ 'mandat]

Okay.

**Dobrze.**
['dɔbʒɛ]

Where are you going?

**Dokąd pan /pani/ jedzie?**
['dɔkɔnt pan /'paɲi/ 'jɛdʑɛ?]

I'm going to ...

**Jadę do ...**
['jadɛ dɔ ...]

How much? I don't understand.

**Ile kosztuje? Nie rozumiem.**
['ilɛ kɔ'ʃtujɛ? ɲɛ rɔ'zumʲɛm]

Write it down, please.

**Czy może pan /pani/ to napisać?**
[tʃɨ 'mɔʒɛ pan /'paɲi/ tɔ na'pʲisatɕ?]

Okay. Can I pay with a credit card?

**Dobrze. Czy mogę zapłacić kartą?**
['dɔbʒɛ. tʃɨ 'mɔgɛ za'pwatɕitɕ 'kartɔ̃?]

Yes, you can.

**Tak, można.**
[tak, 'mɔʒna]

Here's your receipt.

**Oto pański /pani/ rachunek.**
['ɔtɔ 'paɲskʲi /'paɲi/ ra'xunɛk]

Sorry about the fine.

**Przykro mi z powodu mandatu.**
['pʃɨkrɔ mʲi s pɔ'vɔdu ma'ndatu]

That's okay. It was my fault.

**W porządku. To moja wina.**
[f pɔ'ʒɔntku. tɔ 'mɔja 'vʲina]

Enjoy your trip.

**Miłej podróży.**
['mʲiwɛj pɔ'druʒi]

# Taxi

| | |
|---|---|
| taxi | **taksówka**<br>[ta'ksufka] |
| taxi driver | **taksówkarz**<br>[ta'ksufkaʃ] |
| to catch a taxi | **złapać taksówkę**<br>['zwapatɕ ta'ksufkɛ] |
| taxi stand | **postój taksówek**<br>['pɔstuj ta'ksuvɛk] |
| Where can I get a taxi? | **Gdzie mogę wziąć taksówkę?**<br>[gdʑɛ 'mɔgɛ vʑi'ɔ̃tɕ ta'ksufkɛ?] |
| to call a taxi | **zadzwonić po taksówkę**<br>[za'dzvɔɲitɕ pɔ ta'ksufkɛ] |
| I need a taxi. | **Potrzebuję taksówkę.**<br>[pɔtʃɛ'bujɛ ta'ksufkɛ] |
| Right now. | **Jak najszybciej.**<br>['jak na'jʃiptɕɛj] |
| What is your address (location)? | **Skąd pana /panią/ odebrać?**<br>['skɔnt 'pana /'paɲiɔ̃/ ɔ'dɛbratɕ?] |
| My address is … | **Mój adres to …**<br>[muj 'adrɛs tɔ …] |
| Your destination? | **Dokąd pan /pani/ chce jechać?**<br>['dɔkɔnt pa'n /paɲi/ 'xtsɛ 'jɛxatɕ?] |
| Excuse me, … | **Przepraszam, …**<br>[pʃɛ'praʃam, …] |
| Are you available? | **Czy jest pan wolny?**<br>[tʃi 'jɛst pan 'vɔlni?] |
| How much is it to get to …? | **Ile kosztuje przejazd do …?**<br>['ilɛ kɔ'ʃtujɛ 'pʃɛjazd dɔ …?] |
| Do you know where it is? | **Wie pan /pani/ gdzie to jest?**<br>['vʲɛ pan /'paɲi/ gdʑɛ tɔ 'jɛst?] |
| Airport, please. | **Na lotnisko, proszę.**<br>[na lɔt'ɲiskɔ, 'prɔʃɛ] |
| Stop here, please. | **Proszę się tu zatrzymać.**<br>['prɔʃɛ ɕɛ tu za'tʃimatɕ] |
| It's not here. | **To nie tutaj.**<br>[tɔ ɲɛ 'tutaj] |
| This is the wrong address. | **To zły adres.**<br>[tɔ 'zwi 'adrɛs] |
| Turn left. | **Proszę skręcić w lewo.**<br>['prɔʃɛ 'skrɛntɕitɕ v 'lɛvɔ] |
| Turn right. | **Proszę skręcić w prawo.**<br>['prɔʃɛ 'skrɛntɕitɕ f 'pravɔ] |

How much do I owe you?

**Ile płacę?**
['ilɛ 'pwatsɛ?]

I'd like a receipt, please.

**Poproszę rachunek.**
[po'proʃɛ ra'xunɛk]

Keep the change.

**Proszę zachować resztę.**
['proʃɛ za'xovatɕ 'rɛʃtɛ]

Would you please wait for me?

**Czy może pan /pani/ na mnie poczekać?**
[tʃɨ 'moʒɛ pan /'paɲi/ na mɲɛ po'tʃɛkatɕ?]

five minutes

**pięć minut**
['pʲɛ̃tɕ 'mʲinut]

ten minutes

**dziesięć minut**
['dʑɛɕɛ̃tɕ 'mʲinut]

fifteen minutes

**piętnaście minut**
[pʲɛ'ntnaɕtɕɛ 'mʲinut]

twenty minutes

**dwadzieścia minut**
[dva'dʑɛɕtɕa 'mʲinut]

half an hour

**pół godziny**
['puw go'dʑiɲi]

## Hotel

| | |
|---|---|
| Hello. | **Witam.**<br>['vÍitam] |
| My name is … | **Mam na imię …**<br>[mam na 'imÍiɛ …] |
| I have a reservation. | **Mam rezerwację.**<br>[mam rɛzɛ'rvatsjɛ] |
| I need … | **Potrzebuję …**<br>[pɔtʃɛ'bujɛ …] |
| a single room | **pojedynczy pokój**<br>[pɔjɛ'dɪntʃɪ 'pɔkuj] |
| a double room | **podwójny pokój**<br>[pɔ'dvujnɪ 'pɔkuj] |
| How much is that? | **Ile to kosztuje?**<br>['ilɛ tɔ kɔ'ʃtujɛ?] |
| That's a bit expensive. | **To trochę za drogo.**<br>[tɔ 'trɔxɛ za 'drɔgɔ] |
| Do you have any other options? | **Czy są inne pokoje?**<br>[tʃɪ 'sɔ̃ 'innɛ pɔ'kɔjɛ?] |
| I'll take it. | **Wezmę ten.**<br>['vɛzmɛ 'tɛn] |
| I'll pay in cash. | **Zapłacę gotówką.**<br>[za'pwatsɛ gɔ'tufkɔ̃] |
| I've got a problem. | **Mam problem.**<br>[mam 'prɔblɛm] |
| My … is broken. | **… jest zepsuty /zepsuta/.**<br>[… 'jɛsd zɛ'psutɪ /zɛ'psuta/.] |
| My … is out of order. | **… jest nieczynny /nieczynna/.**<br>[… 'jɛst ɲɛ'tʃɪnnɪ /ɲɛ'tʃɪnna/.] |
| TV | **Mój telewizor …**<br>[muj tɛlɛ'vÍizɔr …] |
| air conditioning | **Moja klimatyzacja …**<br>['mɔja kʎimatɪ'zatsja …] |
| tap | **Mój kran …**<br>[muj 'kran …] |
| shower | **Mój prysznic …**<br>[muj 'prɪʃɲits …] |
| sink | **Mój zlew …**<br>[muj 'zlɛf …] |
| safe | **Mój sejf …**<br>[muj 'sɛjf …] |

| | |
|---|---|
| door lock | **Mój zamek ...**<br>[muj 'zamɛk ...] |
| electrical outlet | **Moje gniazdko elektryczne ...**<br>['mɔjɛ 'gɲaztkɔ ɛlɛ'ktritʃnɛ ...] |
| hairdryer | **Moja suszarka ...**<br>['mɔja su'ʃarka ...] |

| | |
|---|---|
| I don't have ... | **Nie mam ...**<br>[ɲɛ 'mam ...] |
| water | **wody**<br>['vɔdɨ] |
| light | **światła**<br>['ɕvʲatwa] |
| electricity | **prądu**<br>['prɔndu] |

| | |
|---|---|
| Can you give me ...? | **Czy może mi pan /pani/ przynieść ...?**<br>[tʃɨ 'mɔʒɛ mʲi pan /'paɲi/ 'pʃɨɲɛɕtɕ ...?] |
| a towel | **ręcznik**<br>['rɛntʃnik] |
| a blanket | **koc**<br>['kɔts] |
| slippers | **kapcie**<br>['kaptɕɛ] |
| a robe | **szlafrok**<br>['ʃlafrɔk] |
| shampoo | **szampon**<br>['ʃampɔn] |
| soap | **mydło**<br>['mɨdwɔ] |

| | |
|---|---|
| I'd like to change rooms. | **Chciałbym /chciałabym/<br>zmienić pokój.**<br>['xtɕawbɨm /xtɕa'wabɨm/<br>'zmʲɛɲitɕ 'pɔkuj] |
| I can't find my key. | **Nie mogę znaleźć mojego klucza.**<br>[ɲɛ 'mɔgɛ 'znalɛɕtɕ mɔ'jɛgɔ 'klutʃa] |
| Could you open my room, please? | **Czy może pani otworzyć mój pokój?**<br>[tʃɨ 'mɔʒɛ 'paɲi ɔ'tfɔʒɨtɕ muj 'pɔkuj?] |
| Who's there? | **Kto tam?**<br>[ktɔ tam?] |
| Come in! | **Proszę wejść!**<br>['prɔʃɛ 'vɛjɕtɕ!] |
| Just a minute! | **Chwileczkę!**<br>[xvʲi'lɛtʃkɛ!] |
| Not right now, please. | **Nie teraz, proszę.**<br>[ɲɛ 'tɛras, 'prɔʃɛ] |

| | |
|---|---|
| Come to my room, please. | **Proszę wejść do mojego pokoju.**<br>['prɔʃɛ 'vɛjɕtɕ dɔ mɔ'jɛgɔ pɔ'kɔju] |
| My room number is ... | **Mój numer pokoju to ...**<br>[muj 'numɛr pɔ'kɔju tɔ ...] |

I'd like to order food service.

**Chciałbym /chciałabym/ zamówić posiłek do pokoju.**
['xtɕawbɨm /xtɕa'wabɨm/ za'muvʲitɕ pɔ'ɕiwɛg dɔ pɔ'kɔju]

I'm leaving ...

**Wyjeżdżam ...**
[vɨ'jɛʒdʒam ...]

We're leaving ...

**Wyjeżdżamy ...**
[vɨjɛ'ʒdʒamɨ ...]

right now

**jak najszybciej**
['jak na'jʃɨptɕɛj]

this afternoon

**po południu**
[pɔ pɔ'wudɲu]

tonight

**dziś wieczorem**
['dʑiɕ vʲɛ'tʃɔrɛm]

tomorrow

**jutro**
['jutrɔ]

tomorrow morning

**jutro rano**
['jutrɔ 'ranɔ]

tomorrow evening

**jutro wieczorem**
['jutrɔ vʲɛ'tʃɔrɛm]

the day after tomorrow

**pojutrze**
[pɔ'jutʃɛ]

I'd like to pay.

**Chciałbym zapłacić.**
['xtɕawbɨm za'pwatɕitɕ]

Everything was wonderful.

**Wszystko było wspaniałe.**
[fʃɨstkɔ 'bɨwɔ fspa'ɲawɛ]

Where can I get a taxi?

**Gdzie mogę wziąć taksówkę?**
[gdʑɛ 'mɔgɛ vʑi'ɔtɕ ta'ksufkɛ?]

Would you call a taxi for me, please?

**Czy może pan /pani/ wezwać dla mnie taksówkę?**
[tʃɨ 'mɔʒɛ pan /'paɲi/ 'vɛzvatɕ 'dla 'mɲɛ ta'ksufkɛ?]

## Restaurant

| | |
|---|---|
| Can I look at the menu, please? | **Czy mogę prosić menu?**<br>[tʃi 'mɔgɛ 'prɔɕitɕ 'mɛnu?] |
| Table for one. | **Stolik dla jednej osoby.**<br>['stɔʎig 'dla 'jɛdnɛj ɔ'sɔbɨ] |
| There are two (three, four) of us. | **Jest nas dwoje (troje, czworo).**<br>['jɛst 'naz 'dvɔjɛ ('trɔjɛ, 'tʃvɔrɔ)] |
| Smoking | **Dla palących.**<br>['dla pa'lɔntsɨx] |
| No smoking | **Dla niepalących.**<br>['dla ɲɛpa'lɔntsɨx] |
| Excuse me! (addressing a waiter) | **Przepraszam!**<br>[pʃɛ'praʃam!] |
| menu | **menu**<br>['mɛnu] |
| wine list | **lista win**<br>['ʎista 'vʲin] |
| The menu, please. | **Poproszę menu.**<br>[pɔ'prɔʃɛ 'mɛnu] |
| Are you ready to order? | **Czy są Państwo gotowi?**<br>[tʃi 'sɔ̃ 'paɲstfɔ gɔ'tɔvʲi?] |
| What will you have? | **Co Państwo zamawiają?**<br>['tsɔ 'paɲstfɔ zama'vʲajɔ̃?] |
| I'll have ... | **Zamawiam ...**<br>[za'mavʲam ...] |
| I'm a vegetarian. | **Jestem wegetarianinem /wegetarianką/.**<br>['jɛstɛm vɛgɛtaria'ɲinɛm /vɛgɛta'riankɔ̃/] |
| meat | **mięso**<br>['mʲiɛ̃sɔ] |
| fish | **ryba**<br>['rɨba] |
| vegetables | **warzywa**<br>[va'ʒɨva] |
| Do you have vegetarian dishes? | **Czy są dania wegetariańskie?**<br>[tʃi 'sɔ̃ 'daɲa vɛgɛta'riaɲskʲɛ?] |
| I don't eat pork. | **Nie jadam wieprzowiny.**<br>[ɲɛ 'jadam vʲɛpʃɔ'vʲinɨ] |
| He /she/ doesn't eat meat. | **On /Ona/ nie je mięsa.**<br>[ɔn /'ɔna/ ɲɛ 'jɛ 'mʲiɛ̃sa] |

I am allergic to ...

**Jestem uczulony /uczulona/ na ...**
['jɛstɛm utʃu'lɔnɨ /utʃu'lɔna/ na ...]

Would you please bring me ...

**Czy może pan /pani/ przynieść mi ...**
[tʃɨ 'mɔʒɛ pan /'paɲi/ 'pʃɨɲɛɕtɕ mʲi ...]

salt | pepper | sugar

**sól | pieprz | cukier**
['suʎ | 'pʲɛpʃ | 'tsukʲɛr]

coffee | tea | dessert

**kawa | herbata | deser**
['kava | xɛ'rbata | 'dɛsɛr]

water | sparkling | plain

**woda | gazowana | bez gazu**
['vɔda | gazɔ'vana | 'bɛz 'gazu]

a spoon | fork | knife

**łyżka | widelec | nóż**
['wɨʃka | vʲi'dɛlɛts | 'nuʒ]

a plate | napkin

**talerz | serwetka**
['talɛʃ | sɛr'vɛtka]

Enjoy your meal!

**Smacznego!**
[sma'tʃnɛgɔ!]

One more, please.

**Jeszcze raz poproszę.**
['jɛʃtʃɛ 'ras pɔ'prɔʃɛ]

It was very delicious.

**To było pyszne.**
[tɔ 'bɨwɔ 'pɨʃnɛ]

check | change | tip

**rachunek | drobne | napiwek**
[ra'xunɛk | 'drɔbnɛ | na'pʲivɛk]

Check, please.
(Could I have the check, please?)

**Rachunek proszę.**
[ra'xunɛk 'prɔʃɛ]

Can I pay by credit card?

**Czy mogę zapłacić kartą?**
[tʃɨ 'mɔgɛ za'pwatɕitɕ 'kartɔ̃?]

I'm sorry, there's a mistake here.

**Przykro mi, tu jest błąd.**
['pʃɨkrɔ mʲi, tu 'jɛsd 'bwɔnt]

## Shopping

| Can I help you? | **W czym mogę pomóc?**<br>[f 'tʃɨm 'mɔgɛ 'pɔmuts?] |
| --- | --- |
| Do you have ...? | **Czy jest ...?**<br>[tʃɨ 'jɛst ...?] |
| I'm looking for ... | **Szukam ...**<br>['ʃukam ...] |
| I need ... | **Potrzebuję ...**<br>[pɔtʃɛ'bujɛ ...] |

| I'm just looking. | **Tylko się rozglądam.**<br>['tɨlkɔ ɕɛ rɔ'zglɔndam] |
| --- | --- |
| We're just looking. | **Tylko się rozglądamy.**<br>['tɨlkɔ ɕɛ rɔzglɔn'damɨ] |
| I'll come back later. | **Wrócę później.**<br>['vrutsɛ 'puʑɲɛj] |
| We'll come back later. | **Wrócimy później.**<br>[vru'tɕimɨ 'puʑɲɛj] |
| discounts \| sale | **zniżka \| wyprzedaż**<br>['zɲiʃka \| vɨ'pʃɛdaʒ] |

| Would you please show me ... | **Czy może mi pan /pani/ pokazać ...**<br>[tʃɨ 'mɔʒɛ mʲi pan /'paɲi/ pɔ'kazatɕ ...] |
| --- | --- |
| Would you please give me ... | **Czy może mi pan /pani/ dać ...**<br>[tʃɨ 'mɔʒɛ mʲi pan /'paɲi/ datɕ ...] |
| Can I try it on? | **Czy mogę przymierzyć?**<br>[tʃɨ 'mɔgɛ pʃɨ'mʲɛʑɨtɕ?] |
| Excuse me, where's the fitting room? | **Przepraszam,**<br>**gdzie jest przymierzalnia?**<br>[pʃɛ'praʃam,<br>gdʑɛ 'jɛst pʃɨmʲɛ'ʑalɲa?] |
| Which color would you like? | **Jaki kolor pan /pani/ sobie życzy?**<br>['jakʲi 'kɔlɔr pan /'paɲi/ 'sɔbʲɛ 'ʑɨtʃɨ?] |
| size \| length | **rozmiar \| długość**<br>['rɔzmʲar \| 'dwugɔɕtɕ] |
| How does it fit? | **Jak to leży?**<br>['jak tɔ 'lɛʑɨ?] |

| How much is it? | **Ile to kosztuje?**<br>['ilɛ tɔ kɔ'ʃtujɛ?] |
| --- | --- |
| That's too expensive. | **To za drogo.**<br>[tɔ za 'drɔgɔ] |
| I'll take it. | **Wezmę to.**<br>['vɛzmɛ 'tɔ] |

| | |
|---|---|
| Excuse me, where do I pay? | **Przepraszam, gdzie mogę zapłacić?**<br>[pʃɛ'praʃam, gdʑɛ 'mɔgɛ za'pwatɕitɕ?] |
| Will you pay in cash or credit card? | **Czy płaci pan /pani/**<br>**gotówką czy kartą?**<br>[ʧi 'pwatɕi pan /'paɲi/<br>gɔ'tufkɔ̃ ʧi 'kartɔ̃?] |
| In cash \| with credit card | **Gotówką \| kartą kredytową**<br>[gɔ'tufkɔ̃ \| 'kartɔ̃ krɛdɨ'tɔvɔ̃] |

| | |
|---|---|
| Do you want the receipt? | **Czy chce pan /pani/ rachunek?**<br>[ʧi xtsɛ pan /'paɲi/ ra'xunɛk?] |
| Yes, please. | **Tak, proszę.**<br>[tak, 'prɔʃɛ] |
| No, it's OK. | **Nie, dziękuję.**<br>[ɲɛ, dʑiɛ'ŋkujɛ] |
| Thank you. Have a nice day! | **Dziękuję. Miłego dnia!**<br>[dʑiɛŋ'kujɛ. mʲi'wɛgɔ dɲa!] |

# In town

| | |
|---|---|
| Excuse me, please. | **Przepraszam.**<br>[pʃɛ'praʃam] |
| I'm looking for … | **Szukam …**<br>['ʃukam …] |
| the subway | **metra**<br>['mɛtra] |
| my hotel | **mojego hotelu**<br>[mɔ'jɛgɔ xɔ'tɛlu] |
| the movie theater | **kina**<br>['kʲina] |
| a taxi stand | **postoju taksówek**<br>[pɔ'stɔju ta'ksuvɛk] |
| an ATM | **bankomatu**<br>[bankɔ'matu] |
| a foreign exchange office | **kantoru wymiany walut**<br>[ka'ntɔru vɨ'mʲanɨ va'lut] |
| an internet café | **kafejki internetowej**<br>[ka'fɛjkʲi intɛrnɛ'tɔvɛj] |
| … street | **ulicy …**<br>[u'ʎitsɨ …] |
| this place | **tego miejsca**<br>['tɛgɔ 'mʲɛjstsa] |
| Do you know where … is? | **Czy wie pan /pani/ gdzie jest …?**<br>[tʃɨ 'vʲɛ pan /'paɲi/ gdʑɛ 'jɛst …?] |
| Which street is this? | **Na jakiej to ulicy?**<br>[na 'jakʲɛj tɔ u'ʎitsɨ?] |
| Show me where we are right now. | **Proszę mi pokazać**<br>**gdzie teraz jesteśmy.**<br>['prɔʃɛ mʲi pɔ'kazatɕ<br>gdʑɛ 'tɛras jɛ'stɛɕmɨ] |
| Can I get there on foot? | **Czy mogę tam dojść pieszo?**<br>[tʃɨ 'mɔgɛ tam 'dɔjɕtɕ 'pʲɛʃɔ?] |
| Do you have a map of the city? | **Czy ma pan /pani/ mapę miasta?**<br>[tʃɨ ma pan /'paɲi/ 'mapɛ 'mʲasta?] |
| How much is a ticket to get in? | **Ile kosztuje wejście?**<br>['ilɛ kɔ'ʃtujɛ 'vɛjɕtɕɛ?] |
| Can I take pictures here? | **Czy można tu robić zdjęcia?**<br>[tʃɨ 'mɔʒna tu 'rɔbʲitɕ 'zdjɛntɕa?] |
| Are you open? | **Czy jest otwarte?**<br>[tʃɨ 'jɛst ɔ'tfartɛ?] |

When do you open?

**Od której jest czynne?**
[ɔt 'kturɛj 'jɛst 'ʧinnɛ?]

When do you close?

**Do której jest czynne?**
[dɔ 'kturɛj 'jɛst 'ʧinnɛ?]

# Money

| | |
|---|---|
| money | **pieniądze** [pʲɛ'nʲɔndzɛ] |
| cash | **gotówka** [gɔ'tufka] |
| paper money | **pieniądze papierowe** [pʲɛ'nʲɔndzɛ papʲɛ'rɔvɛ] |
| loose change | **drobne** ['drɔbnɛ] |
| check \| change \| tip | **rachunek \| drobne \| napiwek** [ra'xunɛk \| 'drɔbnɛ \| na'pʲivɛk] |
| credit card | **karta kredytowa** ['karta krɛdɨ'tɔva] |
| wallet | **portfel** ['pɔrtfɛl] |
| to buy | **kupować** [ku'pɔvatɕ] |
| to pay | **płacić** ['pwatɕitɕ] |
| fine | **grzywna** ['gʒɨvna] |
| free | **darmowy** [da'rmɔvɨ] |
| Where can I buy ...? | **Gdzie mogę kupić ...?** [gdʑɛ 'mɔgɛ 'kupʲitɕ ...?] |
| Is the bank open now? | **Czy bank jest teraz otwarty?** [tʃɨ 'bank 'jɛst 'tɛraz ɔ'tfartɨ?] |
| When does it open? | **Od której jest czynny?** [ɔt 'kturɛj 'jɛst 'tʃɨnnɨ?] |
| When does it close? | **Do której jest czynny?** [dɔ 'kturɛj 'jɛst 'tʃɨnnɨ?] |
| How much? | **Ile kosztuje?** ['ilɛ kɔ'ʃtujɛ?] |
| How much is this? | **Ile to kosztuje?** ['ilɛ tɔ kɔ'ʃtujɛ?] |
| That's too expensive. | **To za drogo.** [tɔ za 'drɔgɔ] |
| Excuse me, where do I pay? | **Przepraszam, gdzie mogę zapłacić?** [pʃɛ'praʃam, gdʑɛ 'mɔgɛ za'pwatɕitɕ?] |
| Check, please. | **Rachunek proszę.** [ra'xunɛk 'prɔʃɛ] |

| | |
|---|---|
| Can I pay by credit card? | **Czy mogę zapłacić kartą?**<br>[tʃi 'mɔgɛ za'pwatɕitɕ 'kartɔ̃?] |
| Is there an ATM here? | **Czy jest tu gdzieś bankomat?**<br>[tʃi 'jɛst tu gdʑɛɕ bankɔ'mat?] |
| I'm looking for an ATM. | **Szukam bankomatu.**<br>['ʃukam bankɔ'matu] |

| | |
|---|---|
| I'm looking for a foreign exchange office. | **Szukam kantoru wymiany walut.**<br>['ʃukam ka'ntɔru vi'mʲanɨ 'valut] |
| I'd like to change … | **Chciałbym /Chciałabym/ wymienić …**<br>['xtɕawbɨm /xtɕa'wabɨm/ vi'mʲɛnitɕ …] |
| What is the exchange rate? | **Jaki jest kurs?**<br>['jakʲi 'jɛst 'kurs?] |
| Do you need my passport? | **Czy potrzebuje pan /pani/ mój paszport?**<br>[tʃi pɔtʃɛ'bujɛ pan /'paɲi/ muj 'paʃpɔrt?] |

# Time

| | |
|---|---|
| What time is it? | **Która godzina?**<br>['ktura gɔ'dʑina?] |
| When? | **Kiedy?**<br>['kʲɛdɨ?] |
| At what time? | **O której godzinie?**<br>[ɔ 'kturɛj gɔ'dʑiɲɛ?] |
| now \| later \| after … | **teraz \| później \| po …**<br>['tɛraz \| 'puʑɲɛj \| pɔ …] |

| | |
|---|---|
| one o'clock | **godzina pierwsza**<br>[gɔ'dʑina 'pʲɛrfʃa] |
| one fifteen | **pierwsza piętnaście**<br>['pʲɛrfʃa pʲiɛ'ntnaɕtɕɛ] |
| one thirty | **pierwsza trzydzieści**<br>['pʲɛrfʃa tʃi'dʑɛɕtɕi] |
| one forty-five | **za piętnaście druga**<br>[za pʲiɛ'ntnaɕtɕɛ 'druga] |

| | |
|---|---|
| one \| two \| three | **pierwsza \| druga \| trzecia**<br>['pʲɛrfʃa \| 'druga \| 'tʃɛtɕa] |
| four \| five \| six | **czwarta \| piąta \| szósta**<br>['tʃvarta \| 'pʲiɔnta \| 'ʃusta] |
| seven \| eight \| nine | **siódma \| ósma \| dziewiąta**<br>['ɕudma \| 'usma \| dʑɛ'vʲiɔnta] |
| ten \| eleven \| twelve | **dziesiąta \| jedenasta \| dwunasta**<br>[dʑɛ'ɕiɔnta \| jɛdɛ'nasta \| dvu'nasta] |

| | |
|---|---|
| in … | **za …**<br>[za …] |
| five minutes | **pięć minut**<br>['pʲiɛntɕ 'mʲinut] |
| ten minutes | **dziesięć minut**<br>['dʑɛɕiɛntɕ 'mʲinut] |
| fifteen minutes | **piętnaście minut**<br>[pʲiɛ'ntnaɕtɕɛ 'mʲinut] |
| twenty minutes | **dwadzieścia minut**<br>[dva'dʑɛɕtɕa 'mʲinut] |

| | |
|---|---|
| half an hour | **pół godziny**<br>['puw gɔ'dʑinɨ] |
| an hour | **godzinę**<br>[gɔ'dʑinɛ] |

| | |
|---|---|
| in the morning | **rano**<br>['ranɔ] |
| early in the morning | **wcześnie rano**<br>['ftʃɛɕɲɛ 'ranɔ] |
| this morning | **tego ranka**<br>['tɛgɔ 'ranka] |
| tomorrow morning | **jutro rano**<br>['jutrɔ 'ranɔ] |
| at noon | **w południe**<br>[f pɔ'wudɲɛ] |
| in the afternoon | **po południu**<br>[pɔ pɔ'wudɲu] |
| in the evening | **wieczorem**<br>[vʲɛ'tʃɔrɛm] |
| tonight | **dziś wieczorem**<br>['dʑiɕ vʲɛ'tʃɔrɛm] |
| at night | **w nocy**<br>[f 'nɔtsɨ] |
| yesterday | **wczoraj**<br>['ftʃɔraj] |
| today | **dzisiaj**<br>['dʑiɕaj] |
| tomorrow | **jutro**<br>['jutrɔ] |
| the day after tomorrow | **pojutrze**<br>[pɔ'jutʃɛ] |
| What day is it today? | **Jaki jest dzisiaj dzień?**<br>['jakʲi 'jɛst 'dʑiɕaj 'dʑɛɲ?] |
| It's ... | **Jest ...**<br>['jɛst ...] |
| Monday | **poniedziałek**<br>[pɔɲɛ'dʑawɛk] |
| Tuesday | **wtorek**<br>['ftɔrɛk] |
| Wednesday | **środa**<br>['ɕrɔda] |
| Thursday | **czwartek**<br>['tʃvartɛk] |
| Friday | **piątek**<br>['pʲiɔntɛk] |
| Saturday | **sobota**<br>[sɔ'bɔta] |
| Sunday | **niedziela**<br>[ɲɛ'dʑɛla] |

## Greetings. Introductions

Hello.
**Witam.**
['vʲitam]

Pleased to meet you.
**Miło mi pana /panią/ poznać.**
['mʲiwɔ mʲi 'pana /'paɲiɔ̃/ 'pɔznatɕ]

Me too.
**Mi również.**
[mʲi 'ruvɲɛʒ]

I'd like you to meet …
**Chciałbym żeby pan poznał /pani poznała/ …**
['xtɕawbʲim 'ʒɛbɨ pan 'pɔznaw /'paɲi pɔ'znawa/ …]

Nice to meet you.
**Miło pana /panią/ poznać.**
['mʲiwɔ 'pana /'paɲiɔ̃/ 'pɔznatɕ]

How are you?
**Jak się pan /pani/ miewa?**
['jak ɕɛ pan /'paɲi/ 'mʲɛva?]

My name is …
**Mam na imię …**
[mam na 'imʲiɛ …]

His name is …
**On ma na imię …**
['ɔn ma na 'imʲiɛ …]

Her name is …
**Ona ma na imię …**
['ɔna ma na 'imʲiɛ …]

What's your name?
**Jak pan /pani/ ma na imię?**
['jak pan /'paɲi/ ma na 'imʲiɛ?]

What's his name?
**Jak on ma na imię?**
['jak 'ɔn ma na 'imʲiɛ?]

What's her name?
**Jak ona ma na imię?**
['jak 'ɔna ma na 'imʲiɛ?]

What's your last name?
**Jak pan /pani/ się nazywa?**
['jak pan /'paɲi/ ɕɛ na'zɨva?]

You can call me …
**Może się pan /pani/ do mnie zwracać …**
['mɔʒɛ ɕɛ pa'n /paɲi/ dɔ 'mɲɛ 'zvratsatɕ …]

Where are you from?
**Skąd pan /pani/ jest?**
['skɔnt pan /'paɲi/ 'jɛst?]

I'm from …
**Pochodzę z …**
[pɔ'xɔdzɛ s …]

What do you do for a living?
**Czym się pan /pani/ zajmuje?**
['tʃɨm ɕɛ pan /'paɲi/ zaj'mujɛ?]

Who is this?
**Kto to jest?**
[ktɔ tɔ 'jɛst?]

Who is he?
**Kim on jest?**
['kʲim 'ɔn 'jɛst?]

Who is she?

**Kim ona jest?**
['kʲim 'ɔna 'jɛst?]

Who are they?

**Kim oni są?**
['kʲim 'ɔɲi sɔ̃?]

---

This is ...

**To jest ...**
[tɔ 'jɛst ...]

my friend (masc.)

**mój przyjaciel**
[muj pʃi'jatɕɛl]

my friend (fem.)

**moja przyjaciółka**
['mɔja pʃija'tɕuwka]

my husband

**mój mąż**
[muj 'mɔ̃ʒ]

my wife

**moja żona**
['mɔja 'ʒɔna]

---

my father

**mój ojciec**
[muj 'ɔjtɕɛts]

my mother

**moja matka**
['mɔja 'matka]

my brother

**mój brat**
[muj 'brat]

my sister

**moja siostra**
['mɔja 'ɕɔstra]

my son

**mój syn**
[muj 'sɨn]

my daughter

**moja córka**
['mɔja 'tsurka]

---

This is our son.

**To jest nasz syn.**
[tɔ 'jɛst 'naʃ 'sɨn]

This is our daughter.

**To jest nasza córka.**
[tɔ 'jɛst 'naʃa 'tsurka]

These are my children.

**To moje dzieci.**
[tɔ 'mɔjɛ 'dʑɛtɕi]

These are our children.

**To nasze dzieci.**
[tɔ 'naʃɛ 'dʑɛtɕi]

# Farewells

Good bye!
**Do widzenia!**
[dɔ vʲiˈdzɛɲa!]

Bye! (inform.)
**Cześć!**
[ˈtʃɛɕtɕ!]

See you tomorrow.
**Do zobaczenia jutro.**
[dɔ zɔbaˈtʃɛɲa ˈjutrɔ]

See you soon.
**Na razie.**
[na ˈraʑɛ]

See you at seven.
**Do zobaczenia o siódmej.**
[dɔ zɔbaˈtʃɛɲa ɔ ˈɕudmɛj]

Have fun!
**Bawcie się dobrze!**
[ˈbaftɕɛ ɕɛ ˈdɔbʒɛ!]

Talk to you later.
**Do usłyszenia.**
[dɔ uswiˈʃɛɲa]

Have a nice weekend.
**Miłego weekendu.**
[mʲiˈwɛgɔ vɛɛˈkɛndu]

Good night.
**Dobranoc.**
[dɔˈbranɔts]

It's time for me to go.
**Czas na mnie.**
[tʃas na ˈmɲɛ]

I have to go.
**Muszę iść.**
[ˈmuʃɛ ˈiɕtɕ]

I will be right back.
**Wracam za chwilę.**
[ˈvratsam za ˈxvʲilɛ]

It's late.
**Późno już.**
[ˈpuʑnɔ ˈjuʒ]

I have to get up early.
**Muszę wstać wcześnie.**
[ˈmuʃɛ ˈfstatɕ ˈftʃɛɕɲɛ]

I'm leaving tomorrow.
**Wyjeżdżam jutro.**
[vʲiˈjɛʒdʒam ˈjutrɔ]

We're leaving tomorrow.
**Wyjeżdżamy jutro.**
[vʲijɛʒˈdʒamɨ ˈjutrɔ]

Have a nice trip!
**Miłej podróży!**
[ˈmʲiwɛj pɔˈdruʒi!]

It was nice meeting you.
**Miło było pana /panią/ poznać.**
[ˈmʲiwɔ ˈbɨwɔ ˈpana /ˈpaɲiɔ̃/ ˈpɔznatɕ]

It was nice talking to you.
**Miło się rozmawiało.**
[ˈmʲiwɔ ɕɛ rɔzmaˈvʲawɔ]

Thanks for everything.
**Dziękuję za wszystko.**
[dʑɛŋˈkujɛ za ˈfʃɨstkɔ]

| | |
|---|---|
| I had a very good time. | **Dobrze się bawiłem /bawiłam/.**<br>['dɔbʒɛ ɕiɛ ba'vʲiwɛm /ba'vʲiwam/] |
| We had a very good time. | **Dobrze się bawiliśmy.**<br>['dɔbʒɛ ɕiɛ bavʲi'ʎiɕmɨ] |
| It was really great. | **Było naprawdę świetne.**<br>['bɨwɔ na'pravdɛ 'ɕvʲɛtnɛ] |
| I'm going to miss you. | **Będę tęsknić.**<br>['bɛndɛ 'tɛ̃skɲitɕ] |
| We're going to miss you. | **Będziemy tęsknić.**<br>[bɛ'ndʑɛmɨ 'tɛ̃skɲitɕ] |
| Good luck! | **Powodzenia!**<br>[pɔvɔ'dzɛɲa!] |
| Say hi to ... | **Pozdrów ...**<br>['pɔzdruf ...] |

# Foreign language

| | |
|---|---|
| I don't understand. | **Nie rozumiem.**<br>[ɲɛ rɔ'zumʲɛm] |
| Write it down, please. | **Czy może pan /pani/ to napisać?**<br>[tʃi 'mɔʒɛ pan /'paɲi/ tɔ na'pʲisatɕ?] |
| Do you speak ...? | **Czy mówi pan /pani/ po ...?**<br>[tʃi 'muvʲi pan /'paɲi/ pɔ ...?] |

| | |
|---|---|
| I speak a little bit of ... | **Mówię troszkę po ...**<br>['muvʲiɛ 'trɔʃkɛ pɔ ...] |
| English | **angielsku**<br>[a'ngʲɛlsku] |
| Turkish | **turecku**<br>[tu'rɛtsku] |
| Arabic | **arabsku**<br>[a'rapsku] |
| French | **francusku**<br>[fran'tsusku] |

| | |
|---|---|
| German | **niemiecku**<br>[ɲɛ'mʲɛtsku] |
| Italian | **włosku**<br>['vwɔsku] |
| Spanish | **hiszpańsku**<br>[xi'ʃpaɲsku] |
| Portuguese | **portugalsku**<br>[pɔrtu'galsku] |
| Chinese | **chińsku**<br>['xiɲsku] |
| Japanese | **japońsku**<br>[ja'pɔɲsku] |

| | |
|---|---|
| Can you repeat that, please. | **Czy może pan /pani/ powtórzyć?**<br>[tʃi 'mɔʒɛ pan /'paɲi/ pɔ'ftuʒitɕ?] |
| I understand. | **Rozumiem.**<br>[rɔ'zumʲɛm] |
| I don't understand. | **Nie rozumiem.**<br>[ɲɛ rɔ'zumʲɛm] |
| Please speak more slowly. | **Proszę mówić wolniej.**<br>['prɔʃɛ 'muvʲitɕ 'vɔlɲɛj] |

| | |
|---|---|
| Is that correct? (Am I saying it right?) | **Czy jest poprawne?**<br>[tʃi 'jɛst pɔ'pravnɛ?] |
| What is this? (What does this mean?) | **Co to znaczy?**<br>['tsɔ tɔ 'znatʃi?] |

## Apologies

| | |
|---|---|
| Excuse me, please. | **Przepraszam.**<br>[pʃɛ'praʃam] |
| I'm sorry. | **Przepraszam.**<br>[pʃɛ'praʃam] |
| I'm really sorry. | **Bardzo przepraszam.**<br>['bardzɔ pʃɛ'praʃam] |
| Sorry, it's my fault. | **Przepraszam, to moja wina.**<br>[pʃɛ'praʃam, tɔ 'mɔja 'vʲina] |
| My mistake. | **Mój błąd.**<br>[muj 'bwɔnt] |

| | |
|---|---|
| May I ...? | **Czy mogę ...?**<br>[ʧɨ 'mɔgɛ ...?] |
| Do you mind if I ...? | **Czy ma pan /pani/<br>coś przeciwko gdybym ...?**<br>[ʧɨ ma pan /'paɲi/<br>'tsɔɕ pʃɛ'tɕifkɔ 'gdɨbɨm ...?] |

| | |
|---|---|
| It's OK. | **Nic się nie stało.**<br>['ɲits ɕɛ̇ ɲɛ 'stawɔ] |
| It's all right. | **Wszystko w porządku.**<br>['fʃɨstkɔ f pɔ'ʒɔntku] |
| Don't worry about it. | **Nic nie szkodzi.**<br>['ɲits ɲɛ 'ʃkɔdʑi] |

# Agreement

| Yes. | **Tak.** |
| | [tak] |
| Yes, sure. | **Tak, oczywiście.** |
| | [tak, ɔtʃiˈvʲiɕtɕɛ] |
| OK (Good!) | **Dobrze!** |
| | [ˈdɔbʒɛ!] |
| Very well. | **Bardzo dobrze.** |
| | [ˈbardzɔ ˈdɔbʒɛ] |
| Certainly! | **Oczywiście!** |
| | [ɔtʃiˈvʲiɕtɕɛ!] |
| I agree. | **Zgadzam się.** |
| | [ˈzgadzam ɕɛ] |

| That's correct. | **Dokładnie tak.** |
| | [dɔˈkwadɲɛ ˈtak] |
| That's right. | **Zgadza się.** |
| | [ˈzgadza ɕɛ] |
| You're right. | **Ma pan /pani/ rację.** |
| | [ma pan /ˈpaɲi/ ˈratsjɛ] |
| I don't mind. | **Nie mam nic przeciwko.** |
| | [ɲɛ ˈmam ˈɲits pʃɛˈtɕifkɔ] |
| Absolutely right. | **Bardzo poprawnie.** |
| | [ˈbardzɔ pɔˈpravɲɛ] |

| It's possible. | **To możliwe.** |
| | [tɔ mɔˈʒʎivɛ] |
| That's a good idea. | **To dobry pomysł.** |
| | [tɔ ˈdɔbri ˈpomis] |
| I can't say no. | **Nie mogę odmówić.** |
| | [ɲɛ ˈmɔgɛ ɔˈdmuvʲitɕ] |
| I'd be happy to. | **Z radością.** |
| | [z raˈdɔɕtɕɔ̃] |
| With pleasure. | **Z przyjemnością.** |
| | [s pʃijɛˈmnɔɕtɕɔ̃] |

## Refusal. Expressing doubt

| | |
|---|---|
| No. | **Nie.**<br>[ɲɛ] |
| Certainly not. | **Z pewnością nie.**<br>[s pɛ'vnɔɕtɕɔ̃ 'ɲɛ] |
| I don't agree. | **Nie zgadzam się.**<br>[ɲɛ 'zgadzam ɕɛ] |
| I don't think so. | **Nie wydaje mi się.**<br>[ɲɛ vɨ'dajɛ mʲi ɕɛ] |
| It's not true. | **To nie prawda.**<br>[tɔ ɲɛ 'pravda] |
| You are wrong. | **Nie ma pan /pani/ racji.**<br>[ɲɛ ma pan /'paɲi/ 'ratsji] |
| I think you are wrong. | **Myślę że nie ma pan /pani/ racji.**<br>['mɨɕlɛ 'ʐɛ ɲɛ ma pan /'paɲi/ 'ratsji] |
| I'm not sure. | **Nie jestem pewien /pewna/.**<br>[ɲɛ 'jɛstɛm 'pɛvʲɛn /'pɛvna/] |
| It's impossible. | **To niemożliwe.**<br>[tɔ ɲɛmɔ'ʐʎivɛ] |
| Nothing of the kind (sort)! | **Nic podobnego!**<br>['ɲits pɔdɔ'bnɛgɔ!] |
| The exact opposite. | **Dokładnie odwrotnie.**<br>[dɔ'kwadɲɛ ɔ'dvrɔtɲɛ] |
| I'm against it. | **Nie zgadzam się.**<br>[ɲɛ 'zgadzam ɕɛ] |
| I don't care. | **Wszystko mi jedno.**<br>['fʃɨstkɔ mʲi 'jɛdnɔ] |
| I have no idea. | **Nie mam pojęcia.**<br>[ɲɛ 'mam pɔ'jɛntɕa] |
| I doubt that. | **Wątpię w to.**<br>['vɔntpʲɛ f 'tɔ] |
| Sorry, I can't. | **Przepraszam, nie mogę.**<br>[pʃɛ'praʃam, ɲɛ 'mɔgɛ] |
| Sorry, I don't want to. | **Przepraszam, nie chcę.**<br>[pʃɛ'praʃam, ɲɛ 'xtsɛ] |
| Thank you, but I don't need this. | **Dziękuję, ale nie potrzebuję tego.**<br>[dʑiɛŋ'kujɛ, 'alɛ ɲɛ pɔtʃɛ'bujɛ 'tɛgɔ] |
| It's late. | **Robi się późno.**<br>['rɔbʲi ɕɛ 'puʐnɔ] |

I have to get up early.

**Muszę wstać wcześnie.**
['muʃɛ 'fstatɕ 'ftʃɛɕɲɛ]

I don't feel well.

**Źle się czuję.**
[ʑlɛ ɕɛ 'tʃujɛ]

# Expressing gratitude

| | |
|---|---|
| Thank you. | **Dziękuję.**<br>[dʑɛɲ'kujɛ] |
| Thank you very much. | **Dziękuję bardzo.**<br>[dʑɛɲ'kujɛ 'bardzɔ] |

| | |
|---|---|
| I really appreciate it. | **Naprawdę to doceniam.**<br>[na'pravdɛ tɔ dɔ'tsɛɲam] |
| I'm really grateful to you. | **Jestem naprawdę wdzięczny**<br>**/wdzięczna/.**<br>['jɛstɛm na'pravdɛ 'vdʑɛntʃɲi<br>/'vdʑɛntʃna/] |
| We are really grateful to you. | **Jesteśmy naprawdę wdzięczni.**<br>[jɛs'tɛɕmɨ na'pravdɛ 'vdʑɛntʃɲi] |

| | |
|---|---|
| Thank you for your time. | **Dziękuję za poświęcony czas.**<br>[dʑɛɲ'kujɛ za pɔɕvʲɛn'tsɔnɨ 'tʃas] |
| Thanks for everything. | **Dziękuję za wszystko.**<br>[dʑɛɲ'kujɛ za 'fʃistkɔ] |

| | |
|---|---|
| Thank you for ... | **Dziękuję za ...**<br>[dʑɛɲ'kujɛ za ...] |
| your help | **pańską pomoc**<br>['paɲskɔ̃ 'pɔmɔts] |
| a nice time | **miłe chwile**<br>['mʲiwɛ 'xvʲilɛ] |

| | |
|---|---|
| a wonderful meal | **doskonałą potrawę**<br>[dɔskɔ'nawɔ̃ pɔ'travɛ] |
| a pleasant evening | **miły wieczór**<br>['mʲiwɨ 'vʲetʃur] |
| a wonderful day | **wspaniały dzień**<br>[fspa'ɲawɨ 'dʑɛɲ] |
| an amazing journey | **miła podróż**<br>['mʲiwa 'pɔdruʒ] |

| | |
|---|---|
| Don't mention it. | **Nie ma za co.**<br>[ɲɛ ma za 'tsɔ] |
| You are welcome. | **Proszę.**<br>['prɔʃɛ] |
| Any time. | **Zawsze do usług.**<br>['zafʃɛ dɔ 'uswuk] |
| My pleasure. | **Cała przyjemność po mojej stronie.**<br>[tsawa pʃɨ'jɛmnɔɕtɕ pɔ 'mɔjɛj 'strɔɲɛ] |

Forget it. It's alright.

**Nie ma o czy mówić.**
[ɲɛ ma ɔ ʧi 'muvʲiʨ]

Don't worry about it.

**Nic nie szkodzi.**
['ɲits ɲɛ 'ʃkɔdʑi]

## Congratulations. Best wishes

Congratulations!
**Gratulacje!**
[gratu'latsjɛ!]

Happy birthday!
**Wszystkiego najlepszego z okazji urodzin!**
[ffʂɨ'stkʲɛgɔ najlɛ'pʃɛgɔ z ɔ'kazji u'rɔdʑin!]

Merry Christmas!
**Wesołych Świąt!**
[vɛ'sɔwɨx 'ɕvʲiɔnt!]

Happy New Year!
**Szczęśliwego Nowego Roku!**
[ʃtʃɛ̃ɕ'ʎi'vɛgɔ nɔ'vɛgɔ 'rɔku!]

Happy Easter!
**Wesołych Świąt Wielkanocnych!**
[vɛ'sɔwɨx 'ɕvʲiɔnt vʲɛlka'nɔtsnɨx!]

Happy Hanukkah!
**Szczęśliwego Chanuka!**
[ʃtʃɛ̃ɕʎi'vɛgɔ 'xanuka!]

I'd like to propose a toast.
**Chciałbym wznieść toast.**
['xtɕawbɨm 'vzɲɛɕtɕ 'tɔast]

Cheers!
**Na zdrowie!**
[na 'zdrɔvʲɛ!]

Let's drink to ...!
**Wypijmy za ...!**
[vɨ'pʲijmɨ za ...!]

To our success!
**Za naszą pomyślność!**
[za 'naʃɔ̃ pɔ'mɨɕlnɔɕtɕ!]

To your success!
**Za Państwa pomyślność!**
[za 'paɲstfa pɔ'mɨɕlnɔɕtɕ!]

Good luck!
**Powodzenia!**
[pɔvɔ'dzɛɲa!]

Have a nice day!
**Miłego dnia!**
['mʲiwɛgɔ 'dɲa!]

Have a good holiday!
**Miłych wakacji!**
['mʲiwɨx va'katsji!]

Have a safe journey!
**Bezpiecznej podróży!**
[bɛ'spʲɛtʃnɛj pɔ'druʑi!]

I hope you get better soon!
**Szybkiego powrotu do zdrowia!**
[ʃɨ'pkʲɛgɔ pɔ'vrɔtu dɔ 'zdrɔvʲa!]

# Socializing

Why are you sad?

**Dlaczego jest pani smutna?**
[dla'tʃɛgɔ 'jɛst 'paɲi 'smutna?]

Smile! Cheer up!

**Proszę się uśmiechnąć,**
**głowa do góry!**
['prɔʃɛ ɕiɛ u'ɕmʲɛxnɔntɕ,
'gwɔva dɔ 'guri!]

Are you free tonight?

**Czy ma pani czas dzisiaj wieczorem?**
[tʃi ma 'paɲi 'tʃaz 'dʑiɕaj vʲɛ'tʃɔrɛm?]

May I offer you a drink?

**Czy mogę zaproponować pani drinka?**
[tʃi 'mɔgɛ zaprɔpɔ'nɔvatɕ 'paɲi 'drinka?]

Would you like to dance?

**Czy mogę prosić do tańca?**
[tʃi 'mɔgɛ 'prɔɕitɕ dɔ 'taɲtsa?]

Let's go to the movies.

**Może pójdziemy do kina?**
['mɔʒɛ pu'jdʑɛmɨ dɔ 'kʲina?]

May I invite you to …?

**Czy mogę zaprosić pani …?**
[tʃi 'mɔgɛ za'prɔɕitɕ 'paɲi …?]

a restaurant

**do restauracji**
[dɔ rɛsta'wratsji]

the movies

**do kina**
[dɔ 'kʲina]

the theater

**do teatru**
[dɔ tɛ'atru]

go for a walk

**na spacer**
[na 'spatsɛr]

At what time?

**O której godzinie?**
[ɔ 'kturɛj gɔ'dʑiɲɛ?]

tonight

**dziś wieczorem**
['dʑiɕ vʲɛ'tʃɔrɛm]

at six

**o szóstej**
[ɔ 'ʃustɛj]

at seven

**o siódmej**
[ɔ 'ɕudmɛj]

at eight

**o ósmej**
[ɔ 'usmɛj]

at nine

**o dziewiątej**
[ɔ dʑɛ'vʲiɔntɛj]

Do you like it here?

**Czy podoba się panu /pani/ tutaj?**
[tʃi pɔ'dɔba ɕiɛ 'panu /'paɲi/ 'tutaj?]

Are you here with someone?

**Czy jest tu pani z kimś?**
[tʃi 'jɛst tu 'paɲi s 'kʲimɕ?]

| | |
|---|---|
| I'm with my friend. | **Jestem z przyjacielem /przyjaciółką/.**<br>['jɛstɛm s pʃija'tɕɛlɛm /pʃija'tɕuwkɔ̃/] |
| I'm with my friends. | **Jestem z przyjaciółmi.**<br>['jɛstɛm s pʃija'tɕuwmʲi] |
| No, I'm alone. | **Nie, jestem sam /sama/.**<br>[ɲɛ, 'jɛstɛm 'sam /'sama/] |

| | |
|---|---|
| Do you have a boyfriend? | **Czy masz chłopaka?**<br>[tʃɨ 'maʃ xwɔ'paka?] |
| I have a boyfriend. | **Mam chłopaka.**<br>[mam xwɔ'paka] |
| Do you have a girlfriend? | **Czy masz dziewczynę?**<br>[tʃɨ 'maʃ dʑɛ'ftʃinɛ?] |
| I have a girlfriend. | **Mam dziewczynę.**<br>[mam dʑɛ'ftʃinɛ] |

| | |
|---|---|
| Can I see you again? | **Czy mogę cię jeszcze zobaczyć?**<br>[tʃɨ 'mɔgɛ tɕɛ 'jɛʃtʃɛ zɔ'batʃitɕ?] |
| Can I call you? | **Czy mogę do ciebie zadzwonić?**<br>[tʃɨ 'mɔgɛ dɔ 'tɕɛbʲɛ za'dzvɔɲitɕ?] |
| Call me. (Give me a call.) | **Zadzwoń do mnie.**<br>['zadzvɔɲ dɔ 'mɲɛ] |
| What's your number? | **Jaki masz numer?**<br>['jakʲi 'maʃ 'numɛr?] |
| I miss you. | **Tęsknię za Tobą.**<br>['tɛ̃skɲɛ za 'tɔbɔ̃] |

| | |
|---|---|
| You have a beautiful name. | **Ma pan /pani/ piękne imię.**<br>[ma pan /'paɲi/ 'pʲiɛŋknɛ 'imʲiɛ] |
| I love you. | **Kocham cię.**<br>['kɔxam tɕɛ] |
| Will you marry me? | **Czy wyjdziesz za mnie?**<br>[tʃɨ 'vɨjdʑɛʃ za 'mɲɛ?] |
| You're kidding! | **Żartuje pan /pani/!**<br>[ʒar'tujɛ pan /'paɲi/!] |
| I'm just kidding. | **Żartuję.**<br>[ʒar'tujɛ] |

| | |
|---|---|
| Are you serious? | **Czy mówi pan /pani/ poważnie?**<br>[tʃɨ 'muvʲi pan /'paɲi/ pɔ'vaʒɲɛ?] |
| I'm serious. | **Mówię poważnie.**<br>['muvʲiɛ pɔ'vaʒɲɛ] |
| Really?! | **Naprawdę?!**<br>[na'pravdɛ?!] |
| It's unbelievable! | **To niemożliwe!**<br>[tɔ ɲɛmɔ'ʒʎivɛ!] |
| I don't believe you. | **Nie wierzę.**<br>[ɲɛ 'vʲɛʒɛ] |
| I can't. | **Nie mogę.**<br>[ɲɛ 'mɔgɛ] |
| I don't know. | **Nie wiem.**<br>[ɲɛ 'vʲɛm] |

| | |
|---|---|
| I don't understand you. | **Nie rozumiem.**<br>[ɲɛ rɔ'zumʲɛm] |
| Please go away. | **Proszę odejść.**<br>['prɔʃɛ 'ɔdɛjɕtɕ] |
| Leave me alone! | **Proszę zostawić mnie w spokoju!**<br>['prɔʃɛ zɔ'stavʲitɕ 'mɲɛ f spɔ'kɔju!] |
| I can't stand him. | **Nie znoszę go.**<br>[ɲɛ 'znɔʃɛ 'gɔ] |
| You are disgusting! | **Jest pan obrzydliwy!**<br>['jɛst pan ɔbʒi'dʎivʲi!] |
| I'll call the police! | **Zadzwonię po policję!**<br>[za'dzvɔɲɛ pɔ pɔ'ʎitsjɛ!] |

# Sharing impressions. Emotions

| I like it. | **Podoba mi się to.**<br>[po'dɔba mʲi ɕiɛ 'tɔ] |
| Very nice. | **Bardzo ładne.**<br>['bardzɔ 'wadnɛ] |
| That's great! | **Wspaniale!**<br>[fspa'ɲalɛ!] |
| It's not bad. | **Nieźle.**<br>['ɲɛʑlɛ] |

| I don't like it. | **Nie podoba mi się to.**<br>[ɲɛ po'dɔba mʲi ɕiɛ 'tɔ] |
| It's not good. | **Nieładnie.**<br>[ɲɛ'wadɲɛ] |
| It's bad. | **To jest złe.**<br>[tɔ 'jɛsd 'zwɛ] |
| It's very bad. | **To bardzo złe.**<br>[tɔ 'bardzɔ 'zwɛ] |
| It's disgusting. | **To obrzydliwe.**<br>[tɔ ɔbʒɨ'dʎivɛ] |

| I'm happy. | **Jestem szczęśliwy /szczęśliwa/.**<br>['jɛstɛm ʃʧɛ̃'ɕʎivɨ /ʃʧɛ̃'ɕʎiva/] |
| I'm content. | **Jestem zadowolony /zadowolona/.**<br>['jɛstɛm zadɔvɔ'lɔnɨ /zadɔvɔ'lɔna/] |
| I'm in love. | **Jestem zakochany /zakochana/.**<br>['jɛstɛm zakɔ'xanɨ /zakɔ'xana/] |
| I'm calm. | **Jestem spokojny /spokojna/.**<br>['jɛstɛm spɔ'kɔjnɨ /spɔ'kɔjna/] |
| I'm bored. | **Jestem znudzony /znudzona/.**<br>['jɛstɛm znu'dzɔnɨ /znu'dzɔna/] |

| I'm tired. | **Jestem zmęczony /zmęczona/.**<br>['jɛstɛm zmɛ'nʧɔnɨ /zmɛ'nʧɔna/] |
| I'm sad. | **Jestem smutny /smutna/.**<br>['jɛstɛm 'smutnɨ /'smutna/] |
| I'm frightened. | **Jestem przestraszony /przestraszona/.**<br>['jɛstɛm pʃɛstra'ʃɔnɨ /pʃɛstra'ʃɔna/] |
| I'm angry. | **Jestem zły /zła/.**<br>['jɛstɛm 'zwɨ /'zwa/] |
| I'm worried. | **Martwię się.**<br>['martfiɛ ɕiɛ] |

I'm nervous.

**Jestem zdenerwowany /zdenerwowana/.**
['jɛstɛm zdɛnɛrvɔ'vani /zdɛnɛrvɔ'vana/]

I'm jealous. (envious)

**Jestem zazdrosny /zazdrosna/.**
['jɛstɛm za'zdrɔsni /za'zdrɔsna/]

I'm surprised.

**Jestem zaskoczony /zaskoczona/.**
['jɛstɛm zaskɔ'tʃɔni /zaskɔ'tʃɔna/]

I'm perplexed.

**Jestem zakłopotany /zakłopotana/.**
['jɛstɛm zakwɔpɔ'tani /zakwɔpɔ'tana/]

## Problems. Accidents

I've got a problem.

**Mam problem.**
[mam 'prɔblɛm]

We've got a problem.

**Mamy problem.**
['mamɨ 'prɔblɛm]

I'm lost.

**Zgubiłem /Zgubiłam/ się.**
[zgu'bʲiwɛm /zgu'bʲiwam/ ɕiɛ]

I missed the last bus (train).

**Uciekł mi ostatni autobus (pociąg).**
['utɕɛk mʲi ɔ'statɲi aw'tɔbus ('pɔtɕiɔŋk)]

I don't have any money left.

**Nie mam ani grosza.**
[ɲɛ 'mam 'aɲi 'grɔʃa]

I've lost my …

**Zgubiłem /Zgubiłam/ …**
[zgu'bʲiwɛm /zgu'bʲiwam/ …]

Someone stole my …

**Ktoś ukradł …**
['ktɔɕ 'ukrat …]

passport

**mój paszport**
[muj 'paʃpɔrt]

wallet

**mój portfel**
[muj 'pɔrtfɛl]

papers

**moje dokumenty**
['mɔjɛ dɔku'mɛnti]

ticket

**mój bilet**
[muj 'bʲilɛt]

money

**moje pieniądze**
['mɔjɛ pʲɛ'ɲiɔndzɛ]

handbag

**moje torebkę**
['mɔjɛ tɔ'rɛpkɛ]

camera

**mój aparat fotograficzny**
[muj a'parat fɔtɔgra'fitʃnɨ]

laptop

**mój laptop**
[muj 'laptɔp]

tablet computer

**mój tablet**
[muj 'tablɛt]

mobile phone

**mój telefon**
[muj tɛ'lefɔn]

Help me!

**Pomocy!**
[pɔ'mɔtsɨ]

What's happened?

**Co się stało?**
['tsɔ ɕiɛ 'stawɔ?]

fire

**pożar**
['pɔʒar]

| | |
|---|---|
| shooting | **strzał**<br>['stʃaw] |
| murder | **morderca**<br>[mɔ'rdɛrtsa] |
| explosion | **wybuch**<br>['vɨbux] |
| fight | **bójka**<br>['bujka] |

| | |
|---|---|
| Call the police! | **Proszę zadzwonić na policję!**<br>['prɔʃɛ za'dzvɔɲitɕ na pɔ'ʎitsjɛ!] |
| Please hurry up! | **Proszę się pospieszyć!**<br>['prɔʃɛ ɕiɛ pɔ'spʲɛʃitɕ!] |
| I'm looking for the police station. | **Szukam komendy policji.**<br>['ʃukam kɔ'mɛndɨ pɔ'ʎitsji] |
| I need to make a call. | **Muszę zadzwonić.**<br>['muʃɛ za'dzvɔɲitɕ] |
| May I use your phone? | **Czy mogę skorzystać z telefonu?**<br>[tʃi 'mɔgɛ skɔ'ʒistatɕ s tɛle'fɔnu?] |

| | |
|---|---|
| I've been … | **Zostałem /Zostałam/ …**<br>[zɔ'stawɛm /zɔ'stawam/ …] |
| mugged | **obrabowany /obrabowana/**<br>[ɔbrabɔ'vanɨ /ɔbrabɔ'vana/] |
| robbed | **okradziony /okradziona/**<br>[ɔkra'dzɔɲi /ɔkra'dzɔna/] |
| raped | **zgwałcona**<br>[zgva'wtsɔna] |
| attacked (beaten up) | **pobity /pobita/**<br>[pɔ'bʲitɨ /pɔ'bʲita/] |

| | |
|---|---|
| Are you all right? | **Czy wszystko w porządku?**<br>[tʃi 'fʃistkɔ f pɔ'ʒɔntku?] |
| Did you see who it was? | **Czy widział pan /widziała pani/ kto to był?**<br>[tʃi 'vʲidʑaw pan /vʲi'dʑawa 'paɲi/ 'ktɔ tɔ 'bɨw?] |
| Would you be able to recognize the person? | **Czy może pan /pani/ rozpoznać sprawcę?**<br>[tʃi 'mɔʒɛ pan /'paɲi/ rɔ'spɔznatɕ 'spraftsɛ?] |
| Are you sure? | **Jest pan pewny /pani pewna/?**<br>['jɛst pan 'pɛvnɨ /'paɲi 'pɛvna/?] |

| | |
|---|---|
| Please calm down. | **Proszę się uspokoić.**<br>['prɔʃɛ ɕiɛ uspɔ'kɔitɕ] |
| Take it easy! | **Spokojnie!**<br>[spɔ'kɔjɲɛ!] |
| Don't worry! | **Proszę się nie martwić!**<br>['prɔʃɛ ɕiɛ ɲɛ 'martfitɕ!] |
| Everything will be fine. | **Wszystko będzie dobrze.**<br>[fʃistkɔ 'bɛndʑɛ 'dɔbʒɛ] |

Everything's all right.

**Wszystko jest w porządku.**
[fʃistkɔ 'jɛsd f pɔ'ʒɔntku]

Come here, please.

**Proszę tu podejść.**
['prɔʃɛ tu 'pɔdɛjɕtɕ]

I have some questions for you.

**Mam kilka pytań.**
[mam 'kʲiʎka 'pɨtaɲ]

Wait a moment, please.

**Proszę chwilę zaczekać.**
['prɔʃɛ 'xvʲilɛ za'tʃɛkatɕ]

Do you have any I.D.?

**Czy ma pan /pani/ dowód tożsamości?**
[tʃɨ ma pan /'paɲi/ 'dɔvut tɔʃsa'mɔɕtɕi?]

Thanks. You can leave now.

**Dziękuję. Może pan /pani/ odejść.**
[dʑiɛn'kujɛ. 'mɔʒɛ pan /'paɲi/ 'ɔdɛjɕtɕ]

Hands behind your head!

**Ręce za głowę!**
['rɛntsɛ za 'gwɔvɛ!]

You're under arrest!

**Jest pan aresztowany
/pani aresztowana/!**
['jɛst pan arɛʃtɔ'vanɨ
/'paɲi arɛʃtɔ'vana/!]

## Health problems

| | |
|---|---|
| Please help me. | **Proszę mi pomóc.**<br>['prɔʃɛ mʲi 'pɔmuts] |
| I don't feel well. | **Źle się czuję.**<br>[ʑlɛ ɕiɛ 'tʃujɛ] |
| My husband doesn't feel well. | **Mój mąż nie czuje się dobrze.**<br>[muj 'mɔ̃ʒ ɲɛ 'tʃujɛ ɕiɛ 'dɔbʒɛ] |
| My son ... | **Mój syn ...**<br>[muj 'sɨn ...] |
| My father ... | **Mój ojciec ...**<br>[muj 'ɔjtɕɛts ...] |
| My wife doesn't feel well. | **Moja żona nie czuje się dobrze.**<br>['mɔja 'ʒɔna ɲɛ 'tʃujɛ ɕiɛ 'dɔbʒɛ] |
| My daughter ... | **Moja córka ...**<br>['mɔja 'tsurka ...] |
| My mother ... | **Moja matka ...**<br>['mɔja 'matka ...] |
| I've got a ... | **Boli mnie ...**<br>['bɔʎi 'mɲɛ ...] |
| headache | **głowa**<br>['gwɔva] |
| sore throat | **gardło**<br>['gardwɔ] |
| stomach ache | **brzuch**<br>['bʒux] |
| toothache | **ząb**<br>['zɔmp] |
| I feel dizzy. | **Kręci mi się w głowie.**<br>['krɛntɕi mʲi ɕiɛ v 'gwɔvʲɛ] |
| He has a fever. | **On ma gorączkę.**<br>[ɔn ma gɔ'rɔntʃkɛ] |
| She has a fever. | **Ona ma gorączkę.**<br>['ɔna ma gɔ'rɔntʃkɛ] |
| I can't breathe. | **Nie mogę oddychać.**<br>[ɲɛ 'mɔgɛ ɔ'ddɨxatɕ] |
| I'm short of breath. | **Mam krótki oddech.**<br>[mam 'krutkʲi 'ɔddɛx] |
| I am asthmatic. | **Jestem astmatykiem.**<br>['jɛstɛm astma'tɨkʲɛm] |
| I am diabetic. | **Jestem diabetykiem.**<br>['jɛstɛm diabɛ'tɨkʲɛm] |

| | |
|---|---|
| I can't sleep. | **Mam problemy ze snem.**<br>[mam prɔ'blɛmɨ zɛ 'snɛm] |
| food poisoning | **Zatrułem się jedzeniem**<br>[za'truwɛm ɕiɛ jɛ'dzɛɲɛm] |

| | |
|---|---|
| It hurts here. | **Boli mnie tu.**<br>['bɔʎi 'mɲɛ 'tu] |
| Help me! | **Pomocy!**<br>[pɔ'mɔtsɨ!] |
| I am here! | **Jestem tu!**<br>['jɛstɛm 'tu!] |
| We are here! | **Tu jesteśmy!**<br>[tu jɛ'stɛɕmɨ!] |
| Get me out of here! | **Wyjmijcie mnie stąd!**<br>[vɨ'jm'ijtɕɛ 'mɲɛ 'stɔnt!] |
| I need a doctor. | **Potrzebuję lekarza.**<br>[pɔtʃɛ'bujɛ lɛ'kaʒa] |
| I can't move. | **Nie mogę się ruszać.**<br>[ɲɛ 'mɔgɛ ɕiɛ 'ruʃatɕ] |
| I can't move my legs. | **Nie mogę się ruszać nogami.**<br>[ɲɛ 'mɔgɛ ɕiɛ 'ruʃatɕ nɔ'gam'i] |

| | |
|---|---|
| I have a wound. | **Jestem ranny /ranna/.**<br>['jɛstɛm 'rannɨ /'ranna/] |
| Is it serious? | **Czy to poważne?**<br>[tʃɨ tɔ pɔ'vaʒnɛ?] |
| My documents are in my pocket. | **Moje dokumenty są w kieszeni.**<br>['mɔjɛ dɔku'mɛntɨ 'sɔ̃ f kʲɛ'ʃɛɲi] |
| Calm down! | **Proszę się uspokoić.**<br>['prɔʃɛ ɕiɛ uspɔ'kɔitɕ] |
| May I use your phone? | **Czy mogę skorzystać z telefonu?**<br>[tʃɨ 'mɔgɛ skɔ'ʒistatɕ s tɛlɛ'fɔnu?] |

| | |
|---|---|
| Call an ambulance! | **Proszę wezwać karetkę!**<br>['prɔʃɛ 'vɛzvatɕ ka'rɛtkɛ!] |
| It's urgent! | **To pilne!**<br>[tɔ 'pʲilnɛ!] |
| It's an emergency! | **To nagłe!**<br>[tɔ 'nagwɛ!] |
| Please hurry up! | **Proszę się pospieszyć!**<br>['prɔʃɛ ɕiɛ pɔ'spʲɛʃitɕ!] |
| Would you please call a doctor? | **Czy może pan /pani/<br>zadzwonić po lekarza?**<br>[tʃɨ 'mɔʒɛ pan /'paɲi/<br>za'dzvɔɲitɕ pɔ lɛ'kaʒa?] |
| Where is the hospital? | **Gdzie jest szpital?**<br>[gdʑɛ 'jɛst ʃpʲi'tal?] |

| | |
|---|---|
| How are you feeling? | **Jak się pan /pani/ czuje?**<br>['jak ɕiɛ pan /'paɲi/ 'tʃujɛ?] |
| Are you all right? | **Czy wszystko w porządku?**<br>[tʃɨ 'fʃistkɔ f pɔ'ʒɔntku?] |

| | |
|---|---|
| What's happened? | **Co się stało?**<br>['tsɔ ɕɛ 'stawɔ?] |
| I feel better now. | **Czuję się już lepiej.**<br>['ʧujɛ ɕɛ 'juʒ 'lɛpʲɛj] |
| It's OK. | **W porządku.**<br>[f pɔ'ʒɔntku] |
| It's all right. | **Wszystko w porządku.**<br>['fʃistkɔ f pɔ'ʒɔntku] |

## At the pharmacy

| | |
|---|---|
| pharmacy (drugstore) | **apteka**<br>[a'ptɛka] |
| 24-hour pharmacy | **apteka całodobowa**<br>[a'ptɛka tsawɔdɔ'bɔva] |
| Where is the closest pharmacy? | **Gdzie jest najbliższa apteka?**<br>[gdʑɛ 'jɛst najb'ʎiʃʃa a'ptɛka?] |

| | |
|---|---|
| Is it open now? | **Czy jest teraz otwarta?**<br>[ʧi 'jɛst 'tɛraz ɔ'tfarta?] |
| At what time does it open? | **Od której jest czynne?**<br>[ɔt 'kturɛj 'jɛst 'ʧinnɛ?] |
| At what time does it close? | **Do której jest czynne?**<br>[dɔ 'kturɛj 'jɛst 'ʧinnɛ?] |

| | |
|---|---|
| Is it far? | **Czy to daleko?**<br>[ʧi tɔ da'lɛkɔ?] |
| Can I get there on foot? | **Czy mogę tam dojść pieszo?**<br>[ʧi 'mɔgɛ tam 'dɔjɕʨ 'pʲɛʃɔ?] |
| Can you show me on the map? | **Czy może mi pan /pani/ pokazać na mapie?**<br>[ʧi 'mɔʒɛ mʲi pan /paɲi/ pɔ'kazaʨ na 'mapʲɛ?] |

| | |
|---|---|
| Please give me something for … | **Proszę coś na …**<br>['prɔʃɛ 'tsɔɕ na …] |
| a headache | **ból głowy**<br>[bul 'gwɔvɨ] |
| a cough | **kaszel**<br>['kaʃɛl] |
| a cold | **przeziębienie**<br>[pʃɛʑiɛm'bʲɛɲɛ] |
| the flu | **grypę**<br>['grɨpɛ] |

| | |
|---|---|
| a fever | **gorączkę**<br>[gɔ'rɔnʧkɛ] |
| a stomach ache | **ból brzucha**<br>[bul 'bʒuxa] |
| nausea | **nudności**<br>[nu'dnɔɕʨi] |
| diarrhea | **rozwolnienie**<br>[rɔzvɔ'lɲɛɲɛ] |
| constipation | **zatwardzenie**<br>[zatfar'dzɛɲɛ] |

| | |
|---|---|
| pain in the back | **ból pleców**<br>[bul 'plɛtsuf] |
| chest pain | **ból w klatce piersiowej**<br>[bul f 'klattsɛ pʲɛ'rɕɔvɛj] |
| side stitch | **kolkę**<br>['kɔʎkɛ] |
| abdominal pain | **ból brzucha**<br>[bul 'bʒuxa] |
| pill | **tabletka**<br>[ta'blɛtka] |
| ointment, cream | **maść**<br>['maɕtɕ] |
| syrup | **syrop**<br>['sirɔp] |
| spray | **spray**<br>['sprai] |
| drops | **drażetki**<br>[dra'ʒɛtkʲi] |
| You need to go to the hospital. | **Musi pan /pani/ iść do szpitala.**<br>['muɕi pan /'paɲi/ 'iɕtɕ dɔ ʃpʲi'tala] |
| health insurance | **polisa na życie**<br>[pɔ'ʎisa na 'ʒitɕɛ] |
| prescription | **recepta**<br>[rɛ'tsɛpta] |
| insect repellant | **środek na owady**<br>['ɕrɔdɛk na ɔ'vadi] |
| Band Aid | **plaster**<br>['plastɛr] |

# The bare minimum

Excuse me, ...

**Przepraszam, ...**
[pʃɛ'praʃam, ...]

Hello.

**Witam.**
['vʲitam]

Thank you.

**Dziękuję.**
[dʑiɛɲ'kujɛ]

Good bye.

**Do widzenia.**
[dɔ vʲi'dzɛɲa]

Yes.

**Tak.**
[tak]

No.

**Nie.**
[ɲɛ]

I don't know.

**Nie wiem.**
[ɲɛ 'vʲɛm]

Where? | Where to? | When?

**Gdzie? | Dokąd? | Kiedy?**
[gdʑɛ? | 'dɔkɔnt? | 'kʲɛdi?]

I need ...

**Potrzebuję ...**
[pɔtʃɛ'bujɛ ...]

I want ...

**Chcę ...**
['xtsɛ ...]

Do you have ...?

**Czy jest ...?**
[tʃi 'jɛst ...?]

Is there a ... here?

**Czy jest tutaj ...?**
[tʃi 'jɛst 'tutaj ...?]

May I ...?

**Czy mogę ...?**
[tʃi 'mɔgɛ ...?]

..., please (polite request)

**..., poproszę**
[..., pɔ'prɔʃɛ]

I'm looking for ...

**Szukam ...**
['ʃukam ...]

restroom

**toalety**
[tɔa'lɛti]

ATM

**bankomatu**
[bankɔ'matu]

pharmacy (drugstore)

**apteki**
[a'ptɛkʲi]

hospital

**szpitala**
[ʃpʲi'tala]

police station

**komendy policji**
[kɔ'mɛndi pɔ'ʎitsji]

subway

**metra**
['mɛtra]

| | |
|---|---|
| taxi | **taksówki**<br>[ta'ksufkʲi] |
| train station | **dworca kolejowego**<br>['dvɔrtsa kɔlɛjɔ'vɛgɔ] |

| | |
|---|---|
| My name is … | **Mam na imię …**<br>[mam na 'imʲiɛ …] |
| What's your name? | **Jak pan /pani/ ma na imię?**<br>['jak pan /'paɲi/ ma na 'imʲiɛ?] |
| Could you please help me? | **Czy może pan /pani/ mi pomóc?**<br>[ʧi 'mɔʒɛ pan /'paɲi/ mʲi 'pɔmuts?] |
| I've got a problem. | **Mam problem.**<br>[mam 'prɔblɛm] |
| I don't feel well. | **Źle się czuję.**<br>[zlɛ ɕiɛ 'ʧujɛ] |
| Call an ambulance! | **Proszę wezwać karetkę!**<br>['prɔʃɛ 'vɛzvaʨ ka'rɛtkɛ!] |
| May I make a call? | **Czy mogę zadzwonić?**<br>[ʧi 'mɔgɛ za'dzvɔɲiʨ?] |

| | |
|---|---|
| I'm sorry. | **Przepraszam.**<br>[pʃɛ'praʃam] |
| You're welcome. | **Proszę bardzo.**<br>['prɔʃɛ 'bardzɔ] |

| | |
|---|---|
| I, me | **ja**<br>['ja] |
| you (inform.) | **ty**<br>['ti] |
| he | **on**<br>[ɔn] |
| she | **ona**<br>['ɔna] |
| they (masc.) | **oni**<br>['ɔɲi] |
| they (fem.) | **one**<br>['ɔnɛ] |
| we | **my**<br>['mɨ] |
| you (pl) | **wy**<br>['vɨ] |
| you (sg, form.) | **pan /pani/**<br>[pan /'paɲi/] |

| | |
|---|---|
| ENTRANCE | **WEJŚCIE**<br>['vɛjɕʨɛ] |
| EXIT | **WYJŚCIE**<br>['vijɕʨɛ] |
| OUT OF ORDER | **NIECZYNNY**<br>[ɲɛ'ʧinni] |
| CLOSED | **ZAMKNIĘTE**<br>[za'mkɲiɛntɛ] |

| OPEN | **OTWARTE**<br>[ɔ'tfartɛ] |
| FOR WOMEN | **PANIE**<br>['paɲɛ] |
| FOR MEN | **PANOWIE**<br>[pa'nɔvʲɛ] |

# CONCISE DICTIONARY

This section contains more than 1,500 useful words arranged alphabetically. The dictionary includes a lot of gastronomic terms and will be helpful when ordering food at a restaurant or buying groceries

**T&P Books Publishing**

# DICTIONARY CONTENTS

T&P Books Publishing

**T&P Books Publishing**

| time | czas (m) | [tʃas] |
|---|---|---|
| hour | godzina (ż) | [gɔ'dʑina] |
| half an hour | pół godziny | [puw gɔ'dʑini] |
| minute | minuta (ż) | [mi'nuta] |
| second | sekunda (ż) | [sɛ'kunda] |

| today (adv) | dzisiaj | ['dʑiɕaj] |
|---|---|---|
| tomorrow (adv) | jutro | ['jutrɔ] |
| yesterday (adv) | wczoraj | ['ftʃɔraj] |

| Monday | poniedziałek (m) | [pɔne'dʑʲawɛk] |
|---|---|---|
| Tuesday | wtorek (m) | ['ftɔrɛk] |
| Wednesday | środa (ż) | ['ɕrɔda] |
| Thursday | czwartek (m) | ['tʃfartɛk] |
| Friday | piątek (m) | [pɔ̃tɛk] |
| Saturday | sobota (ż) | [sɔ'bota] |
| Sunday | niedziela (ż) | [ne'dʑeʎa] |

| day | dzień (m) | [dʑeɲ] |
|---|---|---|
| working day | dzień (m) roboczy | [dʑeɲ rɔ'bɔtʃi] |
| public holiday | dzień (m) świąteczny | [dʑeɲ ɕfɔ̃'tɛtʃni] |
| weekend | weekend (m) | [u'ikɛnt] |

| week | tydzień (m) | ['tidʑeɲ] |
|---|---|---|
| last week (adv) | w zeszłym tygodniu | [v 'zɛʃwim ti'gɔdny] |
| next week (adv) | w następnym tygodniu | [v nas'tɛpnim ti'gɔdny] |

| sunrise | wschód (m) słońca | [fshut 'swɔɲtsa] |
|---|---|---|
| sunset | zachód (m) | ['zahut] |

| in the morning | rano | ['ranɔ] |
|---|---|---|
| in the afternoon | po południu | [pɔ pɔ'wudny] |

| in the evening | wieczorem | [vet'ʃɔrɛm] |
|---|---|---|
| tonight (this evening) | dzisiaj wieczorem | [dʑiɕaj vet'ʃɔrɛm] |

| at night | w nocy | [v 'nɔtsɨ] |
|---|---|---|
| midnight | północ (ż) | ['puwnɔts] |

| January | styczeń (m) | ['stitʃɛɲ] |
|---|---|---|
| February | luty (m) | ['lyti] |
| March | marzec (m) | ['maʒɛts] |
| April | kwiecień (m) | ['kfetʃeɲ] |
| May | maj (m) | [maj] |
| June | czerwiec (m) | ['tʃɛrvets] |

| July | lipiec (m) | ['lipeʦ] |
| August | sierpień (m) | ['ɕerpeɲ] |
| September | wrzesień (m) | ['vʒɛɕeɲ] |
| October | październik (m) | [paʑ'dʑernik] |
| November | listopad (m) | [lis'tɔpat] |
| December | grudzień (m) | ['grudʑeɲ] |

| in spring | wiosną | ['vɔsnɔ̃] |
| in summer | latem | ['ʎatɛm] |
| in fall | jesienią | [e'ɕenɔ̃] |
| in winter | zimą | ['ʒimɔ̃] |

| month | miesiąc (m) | ['meɕɔ̃ʦ] |
| season (summer, etc.) | sezon (m) | ['sɛzɔn] |
| year | rok (m) | [rɔk] |
| century | wiek (m) | [vek] |

## 2. Numbers. Numerals

| digit, figure | cyfra (ż) | ['ʦsifra] |
| number | liczba (ż) | ['liʧba] |
| minus sign | minus (m) | ['minus] |
| plus sign | plus (m) | [plys] |
| sum, total | suma (ż) | ['suma] |

| first (adj) | pierwszy | ['perʃʃi] |
| second (adj) | drugi | ['drugi] |
| third (adj) | trzeci | ['tʃɛtʃi] |

| 0 zero | zero | ['zɛrɔ] |
| 1 one | jeden | ['edɛn] |
| 2 two | dwa | [dva] |
| 3 three | trzy | [tʃi] |
| 4 four | cztery | ['ʧtɛri] |

| 5 five | pięć | [pɛ̃tʃ] |
| 6 six | sześć | [ʃɛɕʧ] |
| 7 seven | siedem | ['ɕedɛm] |
| 8 eight | osiem | ['ɔɕem] |
| 9 nine | dziewięć | ['dʑevɛ̃tʃ] |
| 10 ten | dziesięć | ['dʑeɕɛ̃tʃ] |

| 11 eleven | jedenaście | [edɛ'naɕʧe] |
| 12 twelve | dwanaście | [dva'naɕʧe] |
| 13 thirteen | trzynaście | [tʃi'naɕʧe] |
| 14 fourteen | czternaście | [ʧtɛr'naɕʧe] |
| 15 fifteen | piętnaście | [pɛ̃t'naɕʧe] |

| 16 sixteen | szesnaście | [ʃɛs'naɕʧe] |
| 17 seventeen | siedemnaście | [ɕedɛm'naɕʧe] |

| 18 eighteen | osiemnaście | [ɔɕem'naɕtʃe] |
| 19 nineteen | dziewiętnaście | [dʒevět'naɕtʃe] |

| 20 twenty | dwadzieścia | [dva'dʒeɕtʃʲa] |
| 30 thirty | trzydzieści | [tʃi'dʒeɕtʃi] |
| 40 forty | czterdzieści | [tʃtɛr'dʒeɕtʃi] |
| 50 fifty | pięćdziesiąt | [pě'dʒeɕɔt] |

| 60 sixty | sześćdziesiąt | [ʃɛɕ'dʒeɕɔt] |
| 70 seventy | siedemdziesiąt | [ɕedɛm'dʒeɕɔt] |
| 80 eighty | osiemdziesiąt | [ɔɕem'dʒeɕɔt] |
| 90 ninety | dziewięćdziesiąt | [dʒevě'dʒeɕɔt] |

| 100 one hundred | sto | [stɔ] |
| 200 two hundred | dwieście | ['dveɕtʃe] |
| 300 three hundred | trzysta | ['tʃista] |
| 400 four hundred | czterysta | ['tʃtɛrista] |
| 500 five hundred | pięćset | ['pětʃsɛt] |

| 600 six hundred | sześćset | ['ʃɛɕtʃsɛt] |
| 700 seven hundred | siedemset | ['ɕedɛmsɛt] |
| 800 eight hundred | osiemset | [ɔ'ɕemsɛt] |
| 900 nine hundred | dziewięćset | ['dʒevětʃsɛt] |
| 1000 one thousand | tysiąc | ['tiɕɔts] |

| 10000 ten thousand | dziesięć tysięcy | ['dʒeɕětʃ ti'ɕentsi] |
| one hundred thousand | sto tysięcy | [stɔ ti'ɕentsi] |

| million | milion | ['miʎjɔn] |
| billion | miliard | ['miʎjart] |

## 3. Humans. Family

| man (adult male) | mężczyzna (m) | [měʃt'ʃizna] |
| young man | młodzieniec (m) | [mwɔ'dʒenets] |
| teenager | nastolatek (m) | [nastɔ'ʎatɛk] |
| woman | kobieta (ż) | [kɔ'beta] |
| girl (young woman) | dziewczyna (ż) | [dʒeft'ʃina] |

| age | wiek (m) | [vek] |
| adult (adj) | dorosły (m) | [dɔ'rɔswi] |
| middle-aged (adj) | w średnim wieku | [f 'ɕrɛdnim 'veku] |
| elderly (adj) | w podeszłym wieku | [f pɔ'dɛʃwim 'veku] |
| old (adj) | stary | ['stari] |

| old man | staruszek (m) | [sta'ruʃɛk] |
| old woman | staruszka (ż) | [sta'ruʃka] |
| retirement | emerytura (ż) | [ɛmɛri'tura] |
| to retire (from job) | przejść na emeryturę | ['pʃɛjɕtʃ na ɛmɛri'turě] |
| retiree | emeryt (m) | [ɛ'mɛrit] |

| mother | matka (ż) | ['matka] |
| father | ojciec (m) | ['ɔjtʃɛts] |
| son | syn (m) | [sɨn] |
| daughter | córka (ż) | ['tsurka] |
| brother | brat (m) | [brat] |
| sister | siostra (ż) | ['ɕɔstra] |

| parents | rodzice (l.mn.) | [rɔ'dʒitsɛ] |
| child | dziecko (n) | ['dʒetskɔ] |
| children | dzieci (l.mn.) | ['dʒetɕi] |
| stepmother | macocha (ż) | [ma'tsɔha] |
| stepfather | ojczym (m) | ['ɔjtʃɨm] |

| grandmother | babcia (ż) | ['babtɕa] |
| grandfather | dziadek (m) | ['dʒ'adɛk] |
| grandson | wnuk (m) | [vnuk] |
| granddaughter | wnuczka (ż) | ['vnutʃka] |
| grandchildren | wnuki (l.mn.) | ['vnuki] |

| uncle | wujek (m) | ['vuek] |
| aunt | ciocia (ż) | ['tɕotɕa] |
| nephew | bratanek (m), siostrzeniec (m) | [bra'tanɛk], [sɜst'ʃɛnets] |
| niece | bratanica (ż), siostrzenica (ż) | [brata'nitsa], [sɜst'ʃɛnitsa] |

| wife | żona (ż) | ['ʒɔna] |
| husband | mąż (m) | [mɔ̃ʃ] |
| married (masc.) | żonaty | [ʒɔ'nati] |
| married (fem.) | zamężna | [za'mɛnʒna] |
| widow | wdowa (ż) | ['vdɔva] |
| widower | wdowiec (m) | ['vdɔvets] |

| name (first name) | imię (n) | ['imɛ̃] |
| surname (last name) | nazwisko (n) | [naz'viskɔ] |

| relative | krewny (m) | ['krɛvni] |
| friend (masc.) | przyjaciel (m) | [pʃi'jatʃɛʌ] |
| friendship | przyjaźń (ż) | ['pʃijaʑɲ] |

| partner | partner (m) | ['partnɛr] |
| superior (n) | kierownik (m) | [ke'rɔvnik] |
| colleague | koleżanka (ż) | [kɔle'ʒaŋka] |
| neighbors | sąsiedzi (l.mn.) | [sɔ̃'ɕedʒi] |

## 4. Human body

| organism (body) | organizm (m) | [ɔr'ganizm] |
| body | ciało (n) | ['tɕ'awɔ] |
| heart | serce (n) | ['sɛrtsɛ] |

| blood | **krew** (ż) | [krɛf] |
| brain | **mózg** (m) | [musk] |
| nerve | **nerw** (m) | [nɛrf] |

| bone | **kość** (ż) | [kɔɕtʃ] |
| skeleton | **szkielet** (m) | ['ʃkelet] |
| spine (backbone) | **kręgosłup** (m) | [krɛ̃'gɔswup] |
| rib | **żebro** (n) | ['ʒɛbrɔ] |
| skull | **czaszka** (ż) | ['tʃaʃka] |

| muscle | **mięsień** (m) | ['mẽɲɕɛ̃] |
| lungs | **płuca** (l.mn.) | ['pwutsa] |
| skin | **skóra** (ż) | ['skura] |

| head | **głowa** (ż) | ['gwɔva] |
| face | **twarz** (ż) | [tfaʃ] |
| nose | **nos** (m) | [nɔs] |
| forehead | **czoło** (n) | ['tʃɔwɔ] |
| cheek | **policzek** (m) | [pɔ'litʃɛk] |

| mouth | **usta** (l.mn.) | ['usta] |
| tongue | **język** (m) | ['enzik] |
| tooth | **ząb** (m) | [zɔ̃mp] |
| lips | **wargi** (l.mn.) | ['vargi] |
| chin | **podbródek** (m) | [pɔdb'rudek] |

| ear | **ucho** (n) | ['uhɔ] |
| neck | **szyja** (ż) | ['ʃija] |
| throat | **gardło** (n) | ['gardwɔ] |

| eye | **oko** (n) | ['ɔkɔ] |
| pupil | **źrenica** (ż) | [ʑre'nitsa] |
| eyebrow | **brew** (ż) | [brɛf] |
| eyelash | **rzęsy** (l.mn.) | ['ʒɛnsi] |

| hair | **włosy** (l.mn.) | ['vwɔsi] |
| hairstyle | **fryzura** (ż) | [fri'zura] |
| mustache | **wąsy** (l.mn.) | ['vɔ̃si] |
| beard | **broda** (ż) | ['brɔda] |
| to have (a beard, etc.) | **nosić** | ['nɔɕitʃ] |
| bald (adj) | **łysy** | ['wisi] |

| hand | **dłoń** (ż) | [dwɔɲ] |
| arm | **ręka** (ż) | ['rɛŋka] |
| finger | **palec** (m) | ['palets] |
| nail | **paznokieć** (m) | [paz'nɔketʃ] |
| palm | **dłoń** (ż) | [dwɔɲ] |

| shoulder | **ramię** (n) | ['ramẽ] |
| leg | **noga** (ż) | ['nɔga] |
| foot | **stopa** (ż) | ['stɔpa] |
| knee | **kolano** (n) | [kɔ'ʎanɔ] |

| heel | pięta (ż) | ['penta] |
| back | plecy (l.mn.) | ['pletsi] |
| waist | talia (ż) | ['taʎja] |
| beauty mark | pieprzyk (m) | ['pepʃik] |
| birthmark | znamię (n) | ['znamɛ̃] |
| (café au lait spot) | | |

## 5. Medicine. Diseases. Drugs

| health | zdrowie (n) | ['zdrɔve] |
| well (not sick) | zdrowy | ['zdrɔvi] |
| sickness | choroba (ż) | [hɔ'rɔba] |
| to be sick | chorować | [hɔ'rɔvatʃ] |
| ill, sick (adj) | chory | ['hɔri] |

| cold (illness) | przeziębienie (n) | [pʃɛʒɛ̃'bene] |
| to catch a cold | przeziębić się | [pʃɛ'ʒembitʃ çɛ̃] |
| tonsillitis | angina (ż) | [aɲina] |
| pneumonia | zapalenie (n) płuc | [zapa'lɛne pwuts] |
| flu, influenza | grypa (ż) | ['gripa] |

| runny nose (coryza) | katar (m) | ['katar] |
| cough | kaszel (m) | ['kaʃɛʎ] |
| to cough (vi) | kaszleć | ['kaʃletʃ] |
| to sneeze (vi) | kichać | ['kihatʃ] |

| stroke | wylew (m) | ['vilef] |
| heart attack | zawał (m) | ['zavaw] |
| allergy | alergia (ż) | [a'lergʰja] |
| asthma | astma (ż) | ['astma] |
| diabetes | cukrzyca (ż) | [tsuk'ʃitsa] |

| tumor | nowotwór (m) | [nɔ'vɔtfur] |
| cancer | rak (m) | [rak] |
| alcoholism | alkoholizm (m) | [aʎkɔ'hɔlizm] |
| AIDS | AIDS (m) | [ɛjts] |
| fever | febra (ż) | ['fɛbra] |
| seasickness | choroba (ż) morska | [hɔ'rɔba 'mɔrska] |

| bruise (hématome) | siniak (m) | ['çiɲak] |
| bump (lump) | guz (m) | [gus] |
| to limp (vi) | kuleć | ['kuletʃ] |
| dislocation | zwichnięcie (n) | [zvih'nɛ̃tʃe] |
| to dislocate (vt) | zwichnąć | ['zvihnɔ̃tʃ] |

| fracture | złamanie (n) | [zwa'mane] |
| burn (injury) | oparzenie (n) | [ɔpa'ʒɛne] |
| injury | uszkodzenie (n) | [uʃkɔ'dzɛne] |
| pain | ból (m) | [buʎ] |
| toothache | ból (m) zęba | [buʎ 'zɛ̃ba] |

| to sweat (perspire) | pocić się | ['pɔtʃitʃ ɕɛ̃] |
| deaf (adj) | niesłyszący, głuchy | [neswi'ʃɔ̃tsi], ['gwuhi] |
| mute (adj) | niemy | ['nemi] |

| immunity | odporność (ż) | [ɔt'pɔrnɔɕtʃ] |
| virus | wirus (m) | ['virus] |
| microbe | mikrob (m) | ['mikrɔb] |
| bacterium | bakteria (ż) | [bak'tɛrʰja] |
| infection | infekcja (ż) | [in'fɛkts'ja] |

| hospital | szpital (m) | ['ʃpitaʎ] |
| cure | leczenie (n) | [let'ʃɛne] |
| to vaccinate (vt) | szczepić | ['ʃtʃɛpitʃ] |
| to be in a coma | być w śpiączce | [bitʃ f ɕpɔ̃tʃtse] |
| intensive care | reanimacja (ż) | [rɛani'mats'ja] |
| symptom | objaw (m) | ['ɔbʰjaf] |
| pulse | puls (m) | [puʎs] |

## 6. Feelings. Emotions. Conversation

| I, me | ja | [ja] |
| you | ty | [ti] |
| he | on | [ɔn] |
| she | ona | ['ɔna] |
| it | ono | ['ɔnɔ] |

| we | my | [mi] |
| you (to a group) | wy | [vi] |
| they | one | ['ɔnɛ] |

| Hello! (fam.) | Dzień dobry! | [dʒeɲ 'dɔbri] |
| Hello! (form.) | Dzień dobry! | [dʒeɲ 'dɔbri] |
| Good morning! | Dzień dobry! | [dʒeɲ 'dɔbri] |
| Good afternoon! | Dzień dobry! | [dʒeɲ 'dɔbri] |
| Good evening! | Dobry wieczór! | [dɔbri 'vetʃur] |

| to say hello | witać się | ['vitatʃ ɕɛ̃] |
| to greet (vt) | witać | ['vitatʃ] |
| How are you? | Jak się masz? | [jak ɕɛ̃ maʃ] |
| Bye-Bye! Goodbye! | Do widzenia! | [dɔ vi'dzɛɲa] |
| Thank you! | Dziękuję! | [dʒɛ̃'kue] |

| feelings | uczucia (l.mn.) | [ut'ʃutʃ'a] |
| to be hungry | chcieć jeść | [htʃetʃ eɕtʃ] |
| to be thirsty | chcieć pić | [htʃetʃ pitʃ] |
| tired (adj) | zmęczony | [zmɛ̃t'ʃɔni] |

| to be worried | martwić się | ['martfitʃ ɕɛ̃] |
| to be nervous | denerwować się | [dɛnɛr'vɔvatʃ ɕɛ̃] |
| hope | nadzieja (ż) | [na'dʒeja] |

| to hope (vi, vt) | mieć nadzieję | [metʃ na'dʒeɛ̃] |
| character | charakter (m) | [ha'raktɛr] |
| modest (adj) | skromny | ['skrɔmnɨ] |
| lazy (adj) | leniwy | [le'nivɨ] |
| generous (adj) | hojny | ['hɔjnɨ] |
| talented (adj) | utalentowany | [utalentɔ'vanɨ] |

| honest (adj) | uczciwy | [utʃ'tʃivɨ] |
| serious (adj) | poważny | [pɔ'vaʒnɨ] |
| shy, timid (adj) | nieśmiały | [neɕ'mʲawɨ] |
| sincere (adj) | szczery | ['ʃtʃɛrɨ] |
| coward | tchórz (m) | [thuʃ] |

| to sleep (vi) | spać | [spatʃ] |
| dream | sen (m) | [sɛn] |
| bed | łóżko (n) | ['wuʃkɔ] |
| pillow | poduszka (ż) | [pɔ'duʃka] |

| insomnia | bezsenność (ż) | [bɛs'sɛnɔɕtʃ] |
| to go to bed | iść spać | [iɕtʃ spatʃ] |
| nightmare | koszmar (m) | ['kɔʃmar] |
| alarm clock | budzik (m) | ['budʒik] |

| smile | uśmiech (m) | ['uɕmeh] |
| to smile (vi) | uśmiechać się | [uɕ'mehatʃ ɕɛ̃] |
| to laugh (vi) | śmiać się | ['ɕmʲatʃ ɕɛ̃] |

| quarrel | kłótnia (ż) | ['kwutɲa] |
| insult | zniewaga (ż) | [zni'evaga] |
| resentment | obraza (ż) | [ɔb'raza] |
| angry (mad) | zły | [zwɨ] |

## 7. Clothing. Personal accessories

| clothes | odzież (ż) | ['ɔdʒeʃ] |
| coat (overcoat) | palto (n) | ['paʎtɔ] |
| fur coat | futro (n) | ['futrɔ] |
| jacket (e.g., leather ~) | kurtka (ż) | ['kurtka] |
| raincoat (trenchcoat, etc.) | płaszcz (m) | [pwaʃtʃ] |

| shirt (button shirt) | koszula (ż) | [kɔ'ʃuʎa] |
| pants | spodnie (l.mn.) | ['spɔdne] |
| suit jacket | marynarka (ż) | [mari'narka] |
| suit | garnitur (m) | [gar'nitur] |

| dress (frock) | sukienka (ż) | [su'keŋka] |
| skirt | spódnica (ż) | [spud'nitsa] |
| T-shirt | koszulka (ż) | [kɔ'ʃuʎka] |
| bathrobe | szlafrok (m) | ['ʃʎafrɔk] |
| pajamas | pidżama (ż) | [pi'dʒama] |

| workwear | ubranie (n) robocze | [ub'rane rɔ'bɔtʃɛ] |
| underwear | bielizna (z) | [be'lizna] |
| socks | skarpety (l.mn.) | [skar'pɛti] |
| bra | biustonosz (m) | [bys'tɔnɔʃ] |
| pantyhose | rajstopy (l.mn.) | [rajs'tɔpi] |
| stockings (thigh highs) | pończochy (l.mn.) | [pɔɲt'ʃɔhi] |
| bathing suit | kostium (m) kąpielowy | ['kɔstʲjum kɔ̃pelɔvi] |

| hat | czapka (z) | ['tʃapka] |
| footwear | obuwie (n) | [ɔ'buve] |
| boots (cowboy ~) | kozaki (l.mn.) | [kɔ'zaki] |
| heel | obcas (m) | ['ɔbtsas] |
| shoestring | sznurowadło (n) | [ʃnurɔ'vadwɔ] |
| shoe polish | pasta (z) do butów | ['pasta dɔ 'butuf] |

| cotton (n) | bawełna (z) | [ba'vɛwna] |
| wool (n) | wełna (z) | ['vɛwna] |
| fur (n) | futro (n) | ['futrɔ] |

| gloves | rękawiczki (l.mn.) | [rɛ̃ka'vitʃki] |
| mittens | rękawiczki (l.mn.) | [rɛ̃ka'vitʃki] |
| scarf (muffler) | szalik (m) | ['ʃalik] |
| glasses (eyeglasses) | okulary (l.mn.) | [ɔku'ʎari] |
| umbrella | parasol (m) | [pa'rasɔʎ] |

| tie (necktie) | krawat (m) | ['kravat] |
| handkerchief | chusteczka (z) do nosa | [hus'tɛtʃka dɔ 'nɔsa] |
| comb | grzebień (m) | ['gʒɛbeɲ] |
| hairbrush | szczotka (z) do włosów | ['ʃtʃɔtka dɔ 'vwɔsuv] |

| buckle | sprzączka (z) | ['spʃɔ̃tʃka] |
| belt | pasek (m) | ['pasɛk] |
| purse | torebka (z) | [tɔ'rɛpka] |

| collar | kołnierz (m) | ['kɔwneʃ] |
| pocket | kieszeń (z) | ['keʃɛɲ] |
| sleeve | rękaw (m) | ['rɛ̃kaf] |
| fly (on trousers) | rozporek (m) | [rɔs'pɔrɛk] |

| zipper (fastener) | zamek (m) błyskawiczny | ['zamɛk bwiska'vitʃni] |
| button | guzik (m) | ['guʒik] |
| to get dirty (vi) | wybrudzić się | [vib'rudʒitʃ ɕɛ̃] |
| stain (mark, spot) | plama (z) | ['pʎama] |

## 8. City. Urban institutions

| store | sklep (m) | [sklep] |
| shopping mall | centrum (n) handlowe | ['tsɛntrum hand'lɔvɛ] |
| supermarket | supermarket (m) | [supɛr'markɛt] |
| shoe store | sklep (m) obuwniczy | [sklep ɔbuv'nitʃi] |

| bookstore | księgarnia (z) | [kɕɛ̃'garɲa] |
| drugstore, pharmacy | apteka (z) | [ap'tɛka] |
| bakery | sklep (m) z pieczywem | [sklep s pet'ʃivɛm] |
| candy store | cukiernia (z) | [ʦu'kerɲa] |
| grocery store | sklep (m) spożywczy | [sklep spɔ'ʒivtʃi] |
| butcher shop | sklep (m) mięsny | [sklep 'mensni] |
| produce store | warzywniak (m) | [va'ʒivɲak] |
| market | targ (m) | [tark] |

| hair salon | salon (m) fryzjerski | ['salɔn friz<sup>h</sup>'erski] |
| post office | poczta (z) | ['pɔtʃta] |
| dry cleaners | pralnia (z) chemiczna | ['praʎɲa hɛ'mitʃna] |
| circus | cyrk (m) | [ʦirk] |
| zoo | zoo (n) | ['zɔ:] |

| theater | teatr (m) | ['tɛatr] |
| movie theater | kino (n) | ['kinɔ] |
| museum | muzeum (n) | [mu'zɛum] |
| library | biblioteka (z) | [biblɔ'tɛka] |

| mosque | meczet (m) | ['mɛtʃɛt] |
| synagogue | synagoga (z) | [sɨna'gɔga] |
| cathedral | katedra (z) | [ka'tɛdra] |
| temple | świątynia (z) | [ɕfɔ̃'tiɲa] |
| church | kościół (m) | ['kɔʃtʃɔw] |

| college | instytut (m) | [ins'titut] |
| university | uniwersytet (m) | [uni'vɛrsɨtɛt] |
| school | szkoła (z) | ['ʃkɔwa] |

| hotel | hotel (m) | ['hotɛʎ] |
| bank | bank (m) | [baŋk] |
| embassy | ambasada (z) | [amba'sada] |
| travel agency | agencja (z) turystyczna | [a'gɛnts<sup>h</sup>ja turis'titʃna] |

| subway | metro (n) | ['mɛtrɔ] |
| hospital | szpital (m) | ['ʃpitaʎ] |
| gas station | stacja (z) benzynowa | ['stats<sup>h</sup>ja bɛnzi'nɔva] |
| parking lot | parking (m) | ['parkiŋk] |

| ENTRANCE | WEJŚCIE | ['vɛjɕtʃe] |
| EXIT | WYJŚCIE | ['vijɕtʃe] |
| PUSH | PCHAĆ | [phatʃ] |
| PULL | CIĄGNĄĆ | [tʃɔ̃gnɔɲtʃ] |
| OPEN | OTWARTE | [ɔt'fartɛ] |
| CLOSED | ZAMKNIĘTE | [zamk'nentɛ] |

| monument | pomnik (m) | ['pɔmnik] |
| fortress | twierdza (z) | ['tferʣa] |
| palace | pałac (m) | ['pawaʦ] |
| medieval (adj) | średniowieczny | [ɕrɛdnɔ'vetʃni] |
| ancient (adj) | zabytkowy | [zabit'kɔvi] |

| national (adj) | narodowy | [narɔ'dɔvɨ] |
| well-known (adj) | znany | ['znanɨ] |

## 9. Money. Finances

| money | pieniądze (l.mn.) | [penɔ̃dzɛ] |
| coin | moneta (ż) | [mɔ'nɛta] |
| dollar | dolar (m) | ['dɔʎar] |
| euro | euro (m) | ['ɛurɔ] |

| ATM | bankomat (m) | [ba'ŋkɔmat] |
| currency exchange | kantor (m) | ['kantɔr] |
| exchange rate | kurs (m) | [kurs] |
| cash | gotówka (ż) | [gɔ'tufka] |

| How much? | Ile kosztuje? | ['ile kɔʃ'tue] |
| to pay (vi, vt) | płacić | ['pwatʃitʃ] |
| payment | opłata (ż) | [ɔp'wata] |
| change (give the ~) | reszta (ż) | ['rɛʃta] |

| price | cena (ż) | ['tsɛna] |
| discount | zniżka (ż) | ['zniʃka] |
| cheap (adj) | tani | ['tani] |
| expensive (adj) | drogi | ['drɔgi] |

| bank | bank (m) | [baŋk] |
| account | konto (n) | ['kɔntɔ] |
| credit card | karta (ż) kredytowa | ['karta krɛdi'tɔva] |
| check | czek (m) | [tʃɛk] |
| to write a check | wystawić czek | [vis'tavitʃ tʃɛk] |
| checkbook | książeczka (ż) czekowa | [kɕɔ̃'ʒɛtʃka tʃɛ'kɔva] |

| debt | dług (m) | [dwuk] |
| debtor | dłużnik (m) | ['dwuʒnik] |
| to lend (money) | pożyczyć | [pɔ'ʒɨtʃitʃ] |
| to borrow (vi, vt) | pożyczyć od ... | [pɔ'ʒɨtʃitʃ ɔt] |

| to rent (~ a tuxedo) | wypożyczyć | [vɨpɔ'ʒɨtʃitʃ] |
| on credit (adv) | na kredyt | [na 'krɛdit] |
| wallet | portfel (m) | ['pɔrtfɛʎ] |
| safe | sejf (m) | [sɛjf] |
| inheritance | spadek (m) | ['spadɛk] |
| fortune (wealth) | majątek (m) | [maɔ̃tɛk] |

| tax | podatek (m) | [pɔ'datɛk] |
| fine | kara (ż) | ['kara] |
| to fine (vt) | karać grzywną | ['karatʃ 'gʒɨvnɔ̃] |

| wholesale (adj) | hurtowy | [hur'tɔvi] |
| retail (adj) | detaliczny | [dɛta'litʃnɨ] |

| | | |
|---|---|---|
| to insure (vt) | ubezpieczać | [ubɛs'petʃatʃ] |
| insurance | ubezpieczenie (n) | [ubɛspet'ʃɛne] |
| | | |
| capital | kapitał (m) | [ka'pitaw] |
| turnover | obrót (m) | ['ɔbrut] |
| stock (share) | akcja (ż) | ['aktsʰja] |
| profit | zysk (m) | [zɨsk] |
| profitable (adj) | dochodowy | [dɔhɔ'dɔvɨ] |
| | | |
| crisis | kryzys (m) | ['krizis] |
| bankruptcy | bankructwo (n) | [baŋk'rutstfɔ] |
| to go bankrupt | zbankrutować | [zbaŋkru'tɔvatʃ] |
| | | |
| accountant | księgowy (m) | [kɕɛ̃'gɔvɨ] |
| salary | pensja (ż) | ['pɛnsʰja] |
| bonus (money) | premia (ż) | ['prɛmʰja] |

## 10. Transportation

| | | |
|---|---|---|
| bus | autobus (m) | [au'tɔbus] |
| streetcar | tramwaj (m) | ['tramvaj] |
| trolley bus | trolejbus (m) | [trɔ'lejbus] |
| | | |
| to go by ... | jechać w ... | ['ehatʃ v] |
| to get on (~ the bus) | wsiąść | [fɕɔ̃ctʃ] |
| to get off ... | zsiąść z ... | [zɕɔ̃ctʃ z] |
| | | |
| stop (e.g., bus ~) | przystanek (m) | [pʃis'tanɛk] |
| terminus | stacja (ż) końcowa | ['statsʰja kɔɲ'tsɔva] |
| schedule | rozkład (m) jazdy | ['rɔskwad 'jazdi] |
| ticket | bilet (m) | ['bilet] |
| to be late (for ...) | spóźniać się | ['spuzʲɲatʃ ɕɛ̃] |
| | | |
| taxi, cab | taksówka (ż) | [tak'sufka] |
| by taxi | taksówką | [tak'sufkɔ̃] |
| taxi stand | postój (m) taksówek | ['pɔstuj tak'suvɛk] |
| | | |
| traffic | ruch (m) uliczny | [ruh u'litʃni] |
| rush hour | godziny (l.mn.) szczytu | [gɔ'dʑinɨ 'ʃtʃitu] |
| to park (vi) | parkować | [par'kɔvatʃ] |
| | | |
| subway | metro (n) | ['mɛtrɔ] |
| station | stacja (ż) | ['statsʰja] |
| train | pociąg (m) | ['pɔtʃɔ̃k] |
| train station | dworzec (m) | ['dvɔʒɛts] |
| rails | szyny (l.mn.) | ['ʃinɨ] |
| compartment | przedział (m) | ['pʃɛdʑaw] |
| berth | łóżko (n) | ['wuʃkɔ] |
| airplane | samolot (m) | [sa'mɔlɔt] |
| air ticket | bilet (m) lotniczy | ['bilet lɔt'nitʃi] |

| airline | linie (l.mn.) lotnicze | ['liɲje lɔt'nitʃɛ] |
| airport | port (m) lotniczy | [pɔrt lɔt'nitʃi] |

| flight (act of flying) | lot (m) | ['lɔt] |
| luggage | bagaż (m) | ['bagaʃ] |
| luggage cart | wózek (m) bagażowy | ['vuzɛk baga'ʒɔvi] |

| ship | statek (m) | ['statɛk] |
| cruise ship | liniowiec (m) | [li'ɲjɔveʦ] |
| yacht | jacht (m) | [jaht] |
| boat (flat-bottomed ~) | łódź (ż) | [wuʧ] |

| captain | kapitan (m) | [ka'pitan] |
| cabin | kajuta (ż) | [ka'juta] |
| port (harbor) | port (m) | [pɔrt] |

| bicycle | rower (m) | ['rɔvɛr] |
| scooter | skuter (m) | ['skutɛr] |
| motorcycle, bike | motocykl (m) | [mɔ'tɔʦikʎ] |
| pedal | pedał (m) | ['pɛdaw] |
| pump | pompka (ż) | ['pɔmpka] |
| wheel | koło (n) | ['kɔwɔ] |

| automobile, car | samochód (m) | [sa'mɔhut] |
| ambulance | karetka (ż) pogotowia | [ka'rɛtka pɔgɔ'tɔvʲa] |
| truck | ciężarówka (ż) | [ʧɛ̃ʒa'rufka] |
| used (adj) | używany | [uʒi'vani] |
| car crash | wypadek (m) | [vi'padɛk] |
| repair | naprawa (ż) | [nap'rava] |

## 11. Food. Part 1

| meat | mięso (n) | ['mensɔ] |
| chicken | kurczak (m) | ['kurtʃak] |
| duck | kaczka (ż) | ['katʃka] |

| pork | wieprzowina (ż) | [vepʃɔ'vina] |
| veal | cielęcina (ż) | [ʧelɛ̃'ʧina] |
| lamb | baranina (ż) | [bara'nina] |
| beef | wołowina (ż) | [vɔwɔ'vina] |

| sausage (bologna, pepperoni, etc.) | kiełbasa (ż) | [kew'basa] |

| egg | jajko (n) | ['jajkɔ] |
| fish | ryba (ż) | ['riba] |
| cheese | ser (m) | [sɛr] |
| sugar | cukier (m) | ['ʦuker] |
| salt | sól (ż) | [suʎ] |
| rice | ryż (m) | [riʃ] |
| pasta | makaron (m) | [ma'karɔn] |

| butter | masło (n) śmietankowe | ['maswɔ ɕmeta'ŋkɔvɛ] |
| vegetable oil | olej (m) roślinny | ['ɔlej rɔɕliɲi] |
| bread | chleb (m) | [hlep] |
| chocolate (n) | czekolada (ż) | [tʃɛkɔ'ʎada] |

| wine | wino (n) | ['vinɔ] |
| coffee | kawa (ż) | ['kava] |
| milk | mleko (n) | ['mlekɔ] |
| juice | sok (m) | [sɔk] |
| beer | piwo (n) | ['pivɔ] |
| tea | herbata (ż) | [hɛr'bata] |

| tomato | pomidor (m) | [pɔ'midɔr] |
| cucumber | ogórek (m) | [ɔ'gurɛk] |
| carrot | marchew (ż) | ['marhɛf] |
| potato | ziemniak (m) | [ʒem'ɲak] |
| onion | cebula (ż) | [ʦɛ'buʎa] |
| garlic | czosnek (m) | ['tʃɔsnɛk] |

| cabbage | kapusta (ż) | [ka'pusta] |
| beetroot | burak (m) | ['burak] |
| eggplant | bakłażan (m) | [bak'waʒan] |
| dill | koperek (m) | [kɔ'pɛrɛk] |
| lettuce | sałata (ż) | [sa'wata] |
| corn (maize) | kukurydza (ż) | [kuku'ridʐa] |

| fruit | owoc (m) | ['ɔvɔʦ] |
| apple | jabłko (n) | ['jabkɔ] |
| pear | gruszka (ż) | ['gruʃka] |
| lemon | cytryna (ż) | [ʦit'rina] |
| orange | pomarańcza (ż) | [pɔma'raɲtʃa] |
| strawberry | truskawka (ż) | [trus'kafka] |

| plum | śliwka (ż) | ['ɕlifka] |
| raspberry | malina (ż) | [ma'lina] |
| pineapple | ananas (m) | [a'nanas] |
| banana | banan (m) | ['banan] |
| watermelon | arbuz (m) | ['arbus] |
| grape | winogrona (l.mn.) | [vinɔg'rɔna] |
| melon | melon (m) | ['mɛlɔn] |

## 12. Food. Part 2

| cuisine | kuchnia (ż) | ['kuhɲa] |
| recipe | przepis (m) | ['pʃɛpis] |
| food | jedzenie (n) | [e'dʑɛne] |

| to have breakfast | jeść śniadanie | [eɕtʃ ɕɲa'dane] |
| to have lunch | jeść obiad | [eɕtʃ 'ɔbʲat] |
| to have dinner | jeść kolację | [eɕtʃ kɔ'ʎaʦʰɛ̃] |

| | | |
|---|---|---|
| taste, flavor | smak (m) | [smak] |
| tasty (adj) | smaczny | ['smatʃnɨ] |
| cold (adj) | zimny | ['ʒimnɨ] |
| hot (adj) | gorący | [gɔ'rɔ̃tsɨ] |
| sweet (sugary) | słodki | ['swɔtki] |
| salty (adj) | słony | ['swɔnɨ] |

| | | |
|---|---|---|
| sandwich (bread) | kanapka (ż) | [ka'napka] |
| side dish | dodatki (l.mn.) | [dɔ'datki] |
| filling (for cake, pie) | nadzienie (n) | [na'dʒene] |
| sauce | sos (m) | [sɔs] |
| piece (of cake, pie) | kawałek (m) | [ka'vawɛk] |

| | | |
|---|---|---|
| diet | dieta (ż) | ['dʰeta] |
| vitamin | witamina (ż) | [vita'mina] |
| calorie | kaloria (ż) | [ka'lɔrja] |
| vegetarian (n) | wegetarianin (m) | [vɛgɛtarʰˈjanin] |

| | | |
|---|---|---|
| restaurant | restauracja (ż) | [rɛstau'ratsʰja] |
| coffee house | kawiarnia (ż) | [ka'vʲarɲa] |
| appetite | apetyt (m) | [a'pɛtit] |
| Enjoy your meal! | Smacznego! | [smatʃ'nɛgɔ] |

| | | |
|---|---|---|
| waiter | kelner (m) | ['kɛʎnɛr] |
| waitress | kelnerka (ż) | [kɛʎ'nɛrka] |
| bartender | barman (m) | ['barman] |
| menu | menu (n) | ['menu] |

| | | |
|---|---|---|
| spoon | łyżka (ż) | ['wɨʃka] |
| knife | nóż (m) | [nuʃ] |
| fork | widelec (m) | [vi'dɛlets] |
| cup (e.g., coffee ~) | filiżanka (ż) | [fili'ʒaŋka] |

| | | |
|---|---|---|
| plate (dinner ~) | talerz (m) | ['talɛʃ] |
| saucer | spodek (m) | ['spɔdɛk] |
| napkin (on table) | serwetka (ż) | [sɛr'vɛtka] |
| toothpick | wykałaczka (ż) | [vɨka'watʃka] |

| | | |
|---|---|---|
| to order (meal) | zamówić | [za'muvitʃ] |
| course, dish | danie (n) | ['dane] |
| portion | porcja (ż) | ['pɔrtsʰja] |
| appetizer | przystawka (ż) | [pʃis'tafka] |
| salad | sałatka (ż) | [sa'watka] |
| soup | zupa (ż) | ['zupa] |

| | | |
|---|---|---|
| dessert | deser (m) | ['dɛsɛr] |
| whole fruit jam | konfitura (ż) | [kɔnfi'tura] |
| ice-cream | lody (l.mn.) | ['lɔdɨ] |

| | | |
|---|---|---|
| check | rachunek (m) | [ra'hunɛk] |
| to pay the check | zapłacić rachunek | [zap'watʃitʃ ra'hunɛk] |
| tip | napiwek (m) | [na'pivɛk] |

## 13. House. Apartment. Part 1

| | | |
|---|---|---|
| house | **dom** (m) | [dɔm] |
| country house | **dom** (m) **za miastem** | [dɔm za 'mʲastɛm] |
| villa (seaside ~) | **willa** (ż) | ['viʎa] |
| floor, story | **piętro** (n) | ['pentrɔ] |
| entrance | **wejście** (n) | ['vɛjɕtʃe] |
| wall | **ściana** (ż) | ['ɕtʃʲana] |
| roof | **dach** (m) | [dah] |
| chimney | **komin** (m) | ['kɔmin] |
| attic (storage place) | **strych** (m) | [strɨh] |
| window | **okno** (n) | ['ɔknɔ] |
| window ledge | **parapet** (m) | [pa'rapɛt] |
| balcony | **balkon** (m) | ['baʎkɔn] |
| stairs (stairway) | **schody** (l.mn.) | ['shɔdɨ] |
| mailbox | **skrzynka** (ż) **pocztowa** | ['skʃɨŋka pɔtʃ'tɔva] |
| garbage can | **pojemnik** (m) **na śmieci** | [pɔ'emnik na 'ɕmetʃi] |
| elevator | **winda** (ż) | ['vinda] |
| electricity | **elektryczność** (ż) | [ɛlekt'rɨtʃnɔɕtʃ] |
| light bulb | **żarówka** (ż) | [ʒa'rufka] |
| switch | **wyłącznik** (m) | [vɨ'wɔ̃tʃnik] |
| wall socket | **gniazdko** (n) | ['gɲastkɔ] |
| fuse | **bezpiecznik** (m) | [bɛs'petʃnik] |
| door | **drzwi** (ż) | [dʒvi] |
| handle, doorknob | **klamka** (ż) | ['kʎamka] |
| key | **klucz** (m) | [klytʃ] |
| doormat | **wycieraczka** (ż) | [vɨtʃe'ratʃka] |
| door lock | **zamek** (m) | ['zamɛk] |
| doorbell | **dzwonek** (m) | ['dzvɔnɛk] |
| knock (at the door) | **pukanie** (n) | [pu'kane] |
| to knock (vi) | **pukać** | ['pukatʃ] |
| peephole | **wizjer** (m) | ['vizʰer] |
| yard | **podwórko** (n) | [pɔd'vurkɔ] |
| garden | **ogród** (m) | ['ɔgrut] |
| swimming pool | **basen** (m) | ['basɛn] |
| gym (home gym) | **sala** (ż) **gimnastyczna** | ['saʎa gimnas'tɨtʃna] |
| tennis court | **kort** (m) **tenisowy** | [kɔrt tɛni'sɔvɨ] |
| garage | **garaż** (m) | ['garaʃ] |
| private property | **własność** (ż) **prywatna** | ['vwasnɔɕtʃ prɨ'vatna] |
| warning sign | **tabliczka** (ż) **ostrzegawcza** | [tab'litʃka ɔstʃɛ'gaftʃa] |
| security | **ochrona** (ż) | [ɔh'rɔna] |

| | | |
|---|---|---|
| security guard | ochroniarz (m) | [ɔh'rɔɲaʃ] |
| renovations | remont (m) | ['rɛmɔnt] |
| to renovate (vt) | robić remont | ['rɔbitʃ 'rɛmɔnt] |
| to put in order | doprowadzać do porządku | [dɔprɔ'vadzatʃ dɔ pɔ'ʒɔ̃tku] |
| to paint (~ a wall) | malować | [ma'lɔvatʃ] |
| wallpaper | tapety (l.mn.) | [ta'pɛti] |
| to varnish (vt) | lakierować | [ʎake'rɔvatʃ] |
| pipe | rura (ż) | ['rura] |
| tools | narzędzia (l.mn.) | [na'ʒɛ̃dʑia] |
| basement | piwnica (ż) | [piv'nitsa] |
| sewerage (system) | kanalizacja (ż) | [kanali'zatsʰja] |

## 14. House. Apartment. Part 2

| | | |
|---|---|---|
| apartment | mieszkanie (n) | [meʃ'kane] |
| room | pokój (m) | ['pɔkuj] |
| bedroom | sypialnia (ż) | [si'pʲaʎɲa] |
| dining room | jadalnia (ż) | [ja'daʎɲa] |
| living room | salon (m) | ['salɔn] |
| study (home office) | gabinet (m) | [ga'binɛt] |
| entry room | przedpokój (m) | [pʃɛt'pɔkuj] |
| bathroom (room with a bath or shower) | łazienka (ż) | [wa'ʒeŋka] |
| half bath | toaleta (ż) | [tɔa'leta] |
| floor | podłoga (ż) | [pɔd'wɔga] |
| ceiling | sufit (m) | ['sufit] |
| to dust (vt) | ścierać kurz | ['ɕtʃeratʃ kuʃ] |
| vacuum cleaner | odkurzacz (m) | [ɔt'kuʒatʃ] |
| to vacuum (vt) | odkurzać | [ɔt'kuʒatʃ] |
| mop | szczotka (ż) podłogowa | ['ʃtʃɔtka pɔdwɔ'gɔva] |
| dust cloth | ścierka (ż) | ['ɕtʃerka] |
| short broom | miotła (ż) | ['mɔtwa] |
| dustpan | szufelka (ż) | [ʃu'fɛʎka] |
| furniture | meble (l.mn.) | ['mɛble] |
| table | stół (m) | [stɔw] |
| chair | krzesło (n) | ['kʃɛswɔ] |
| armchair | fotel (m) | ['fɔtɛʎ] |
| bookcase | biblioteczka (ż) | [bibʎjɔ'tɛtʃka] |
| shelf | półka (ż) | ['puwka] |
| wardrobe | szafa (ż) ubraniowa | ['ʃafa ubra'nɔva] |
| mirror | lustro (n) | ['lystrɔ] |
| carpet | dywan (m) | ['divan] |

| fireplace | kominek (m) | [kɔ'minɛk] |
| drapes | zasłony (l.mn.) | [zas'wɔnɨ] |
| table lamp | lampka (ż) na stół | ['ʎampka na stɔw] |
| chandelier | żyrandol (m) | [ʒɨ'randɔʎ] |

| kitchen | kuchnia (ż) | ['kuhɲa] |
| gas stove (range) | kuchenka (ż) gazowa | [ku'hɛŋka ga'zɔva] |
| electric stove | kuchenka (ż) elektryczna | [ku'hɛŋka ɛlekt'ritʃna] |
| microwave oven | mikrofalówka (ż) | [mikrɔfa'lyfka] |

| refrigerator | lodówka (ż) | [lɔ'dufka] |
| freezer | zamrażarka (ż) | [zamra'ʒarka] |
| dishwasher | zmywarka (ż) do naczyń | [zmɨ'varka dɔ 'natʃɨɲ] |
| faucet | kran (m) | [kran] |

| meat grinder | maszynka (ż) do mięsa | [ma'ʃɨŋka dɔ 'mensa] |
| juicer | sokowirówka (ż) | [sɔkɔvi'rufka] |
| toaster | toster (m) | ['tɔstɛr] |
| mixer | mikser (m) | ['miksɛr] |

| coffee machine | ekspres (m) do kawy | ['ɛksprɛs dɔ 'kavɨ] |
| kettle | czajnik (m) | ['tʃajnik] |
| teapot | czajniczek (m) | [tʃaj'nitʃɛk] |

| TV set | telewizor (m) | [tɛle'vizɔr] |
| VCR (video recorder) | magnetowid (m) | [magnɛ'tɔvid] |
| iron (e.g., steam ~) | żelazko (n) | [ʒɛ'ʎaskɔ] |
| telephone | telefon (m) | [tɛ'lefɔn] |

## 15. Professions. Social status

| director | dyrektor (m) | [dɨ'rɛktɔr] |
| superior | kierownik (m) | [ke'rɔvnik] |
| president | prezes (m) | ['prɛzɛs] |
| assistant | pomocnik (m) | [pɔ'mɔtsnik] |
| secretary | sekretarka (ż) | [sɛkrɛ'tarka] |

| owner, proprietor | właściciel (m) | [vwaɕ'tʃitʃeʎ] |
| partner | partner (m) | ['partnɛr] |
| stockholder | akcjonariusz (m) | [aktsʰɔ'narʲjuʃ] |

| businessman | biznesmen (m) | ['biznɛsmɛn] |
| millionaire | milioner (m) | [mi'ʎjonɛr] |
| billionaire | miliarder (m) | [mi'ʎjardɛr] |

| actor | aktor (m) | ['aktɔr] |
| architect | architekt (m) | [ar'hitɛkt] |
| banker | bankier (m) | ['baŋker] |
| broker | broker (m) | ['brɔkɛr] |
| veterinarian | weterynarz (m) | [vɛtɛ'rinaʃ] |

| doctor | lekarz (m) | ['lekaʃ] |
| chambermaid | pokojówka (ż) | [pɔkɔ'jufka] |
| designer | projektant (m) | [prɔ'ektant] |
| correspondent | korespondent (m) | [kɔrɛs'pɔndɛnt] |
| delivery man | kurier (m) | ['kurʰer] |

| electrician | elektryk (m) | [ɛ'lektrik] |
| musician | muzyk (m) | ['muzɨk] |
| babysitter | opiekunka (ż) do dziecka | [ɔpe'kuŋka dɔ 'dʒetska] |
| hairdresser | fryzjer (m) | ['friz'er] |
| herder, shepherd | pastuch (m) | ['pastuh] |

| singer (masc.) | śpiewak (m) | ['ɕpevak] |
| translator | tłumacz (m) | ['twumatʃ] |
| writer | pisarz (m) | ['pisaʃ] |
| carpenter | cieśla (m) | ['tʃeɕʎa] |
| cook | kucharz (m) | ['kuhaʃ] |

| fireman | strażak (m) | ['straʒak] |
| police officer | policjant (m) | [pɔ'litsʰjant] |
| mailman | listonosz (m) | [lis'tɔnɔʃ] |
| programmer | programista (m) | [prɔgra'mista] |
| salesman (store staff) | sprzedawca (m) | [spʃɛ'daftsa] |

| worker | robotnik (m) | [rɔ'bɔtnik] |
| gardener | ogrodnik (m) | [ɔg'rɔdnik] |
| plumber | hydraulik (m) | [hid'raulik] |
| dentist | dentysta (m) | [dɛn'tɨsta] |
| flight attendant (fem.) | stewardessa (ż) | [stʰjuar'dɛsa] |

| dancer (masc.) | tancerz (m) | ['tantsɛʃ] |
| bodyguard | ochroniarz (m) | [ɔh'rɔɲaʃ] |
| scientist | naukowiec (m) | [nau'kɔvets] |
| schoolteacher | nauczyciel (m) | [naut'ʃitʃeʎ] |

| farmer | farmer (m) | ['farmɛr] |
| surgeon | chirurg (m) | ['hirurk] |
| miner | górnik (m) | ['gurnik] |
| chef (kitchen chef) | szef (m) kuchni | [ʃɛf 'kuhni] |
| driver | kierowca (m) | [ke'rɔftsa] |

## 16. Sport

| kind of sports | rodzaj (m) sportu | ['rɔdzaj 'spɔrtu] |
| soccer | piłka (ż) nożna | ['piwka 'nɔʒna] |
| hockey | hokej (m) | ['hɔkɛj] |
| basketball | koszykówka (ż) | [kɔʃi'kufka] |
| baseball | baseball (m) | ['bɛjzbɔʎ] |
| volleyball | siatkówka (ż) | [ɕat'kufka] |
| boxing | boks (m) | [bɔks] |

| wrestling | zapasy (l.mn.) | [za'pasɨ] |
| tennis | tenis (m) | ['tɛnis] |
| swimming | pływanie (n) | [pwɨ'vane] |

| chess | szachy (l.mn.) | ['ʃahɨ] |
| running | bieganie (m) | ['begane] |
| athletics | lekkoatletyka (ż) | [lekkɔat'letika] |
| figure skating | łyżwiarstwo (n) figurowe | [wɨʒ'vʲarstfɔ figu'rɔvɛ] |
| cycling | kolarstwo (n) | [kɔ'ʎarstfɔ] |

| billiards | bilard (m) | ['biʎart] |
| bodybuilding | kulturystyka (ż) | [kuʎtu'ristika] |
| golf | golf (m) | [gɔʎf] |
| scuba diving | nurkowanie (n) | [nurkɔ'vane] |
| sailing | żeglarstwo (n) | [ʒɛg'ʎarstfɔ] |
| archery | łucznictwo (n) | [wutʃ'nitstfɔ] |

| period, half | połowa (ż) gry | [pɔ'wɔva grɨ] |
| half-time | przerwa (ż) | ['pʃɛrva] |
| tie | remis (m) | ['rɛmis] |
| to tie (vi) | zremisować | [zrɛmi'sɔvatʃ] |

| treadmill | bieżnia (ż) | ['beʒɲa] |
| player | gracz (m) | [gratʃ] |
| substitute | gracz (m) rezerwowy | [gratʃ rɛzɛr'vovɨ] |
| substitutes bench | ławka (ż) rezerwowych | ['wafka rɛzɛr'vɔvɨh] |

| match | mecz (m) | [mɛtʃ] |
| goal | bramka (ż) | ['bramka] |
| goalkeeper | bramkarz (m) | ['bramkaʃ] |
| goal (score) | bramka (ż) | ['bramka] |

| Olympic Games | Igrzyska (l.mn.) Olimpijskie | [ig'ʒɨska ɔlim'pijske] |
| to set a record | ustanawiać rekord | [usta'navʲatʃ 'rɛkɔrt] |
| final | finał (m) | ['finaw] |
| champion | mistrz (m) | [mistʃ] |
| championship | mistrzostwa (l.mn.) | [mist'ʃɔstva] |

| winner | zwycięzca (m) | [zvɨ'tʃɛnstsa] |
| victory | zwycięstwo (n) | [zvɨ'tʃɛnstfɔ] |
| to win (vi) | wygrać | ['vɨgratʃ] |
| to lose (not win) | przegrać | ['pʃɛgratʃ] |
| medal | medal (m) | ['mɛdaʎ] |

| first place | pierwsze miejsce (n) | ['perfʃɛ 'mejstsɛ] |
| second place | drugie miejsce (n) | ['druge 'mejstsɛ] |
| third place | trzecie miejsce (n) | ['tʃɛtʃe 'mejstsɛ] |

| stadium | stadion (m) | ['stadʰɔn] |
| fan, supporter | kibic (m) | ['kibits] |
| trainer, coach | trener (m) | ['trɛnɛr] |
| training | trening (m) | ['trɛniŋk] |

## 17. Foreign languages. Orthography

| language | język (m) | ['enzik] |
| to study (vt) | studiować | [stud<sup>h</sup>ɔvatʃ] |
| pronunciation | wymowa (ż) | [vi'mɔva] |
| accent | akcent (m) | ['aktsɛnt] |

| noun | rzeczownik (m) | [ʒɛt'ʃɔvnik] |
| adjective | przymiotnik (m) | [pʃi'mɜtnik] |
| verb | czasownik (m) | [tʃa'sɔvnik] |
| adverb | przysłówek (m) | [pʃis'wuvɛk] |

| pronoun | zaimek (m) | [za'imɛk] |
| interjection | wykrzyknik (m) | [vik'ʃiknik] |
| preposition | przyimek (m) | [pʃi'imɛk] |

| root | rdzeń (m) słowa | [rdzɛɲ 'swɔva] |
| ending | końcówka (ż) | [kɔɲ'tsufka] |
| prefix | prefiks (m) | ['prɛfiks] |
| syllable | sylaba (ż) | [si'ʎaba] |
| suffix | sufiks (m) | ['sufiks] |

| stress mark | akcent (m) | ['aktsɛnt] |
| period, dot | kropka (ż) | ['krɔpka] |
| comma | przecinek (m) | [pʃɛ'tʃinɛk] |
| colon | dwukropek (m) | [dvuk'rɔpɛk] |
| ellipsis | wielokropek (m) | [vɛlɜk'rɔpɛk] |

| question | pytanie (n) | [pi'tane] |
| question mark | znak (m) zapytania | [znak zapi'taɲa] |
| exclamation point | wykrzyknik (m) | [vik'ʃiknik] |

| in quotation marks | w cudzysłowie | [f tsudzis'wɔve] |
| in parenthesis | w nawiasie | [v na'vʲaɕe] |
| letter | litera (ż) | [li'tɛra] |
| capital letter | wielka litera (ż) | ['vɛʎka li'tɛra] |

| sentence | zdanie (n) | ['zdane] |
| group of words | połączenie (n) wyrazowe | [pɔwɔ̃t'ʃene vira'zɔvɛ] |
| expression | wyrażenie (n) | [vira'ʒɛne] |

| subject | podmiot (m) | ['pɔdmɜt] |
| predicate | orzeczenie (n) | [ɔʒɛt'ʃɛne] |
| line | linijka (n) | [li'nijka] |
| paragraph | akapit (m) | [a'kapit] |

| synonym | synonim (m) | [si'nɔnim] |
| antonym | antonim (m) | [an'tɔnim] |
| exception | wyjątek (m) | [viɜ̃tɛk] |
| to underline (vt) | podkreślić | [pɔtk'rɛɕlitʃ] |
| rules | reguły (l.mn.) | [rɛ'guwi] |

| grammar | gramatyka (ż) | [gra'matika] |
| vocabulary | słownictwo (n) | [swɔv'nitstfɔ] |
| phonetics | fonetyka (ż) | [fɔ'nɛtika] |
| alphabet | alfabet (m) | [aʎ'fabɛt] |

| textbook | podręcznik (m) | [pɔd'rɛntʃnik] |
| dictionary | słownik (m) | ['swɔvnik] |
| phrasebook | rozmówki (l.mn.) | [rɔz'mufki] |

| word | wyraz (m), słowo (n) | ['viras], ['svɔvɔ] |
| meaning | znaczenie (n) | [zna'tʃɛnie] |
| memory | pamięć (ż) | ['pamɛ̃tʃ] |

## 18. The Earth. Geography

| the Earth | Ziemia (ż) | ['ʒemʲa] |
| the globe (the Earth) | kula (ż) ziemska | ['kuʎa 'ʒemska] |
| planet | planeta (ż) | [pʎa'nɛta] |

| geography | geografia (ż) | [gɛɔg'rafʲja] |
| nature | przyroda (ż) | [pʃi'rɔda] |
| map | mapa (ż) | ['mapa] |
| atlas | atlas (m) | ['atʎas] |

| in the north | na północy | [na puw'nɔtsi] |
| in the south | na południu | [na pɔ'wudny] |
| in the west | na zachodzie | [na za'hɔdʒe] |
| in the east | na wschodzie | [na 'fshɔdʒe] |

| sea | morze (n) | ['mɔʒɛ] |
| ocean | ocean (m) | [ɔ'tsɛan] |
| gulf (bay) | zatoka (ż) | [za'tɔka] |
| straits | cieśnina (ż) | [tʃeɕ'nina] |

| continent (mainland) | kontynent (m) | [kɔn'tinɛnt] |
| island | wyspa (ż) | ['vispa] |
| peninsula | półwysep (m) | [puw'visɛp] |
| archipelago | archipelag (m) | [arhi'pɛʎak] |

| harbor | port (m) | [pɔrt] |
| coral reef | rafa (ż) koralowa | ['rafa kɔra'lɔva] |
| shore | brzeg (m) | [bʒɛk] |
| coast | wybrzeże (n) | [vib'ʒɛʒe] |

| flow (flood tide) | przypływ (m) | ['pʃipwif] |
| ebb (ebb tide) | odpływ (m) | ['ɔtpwif] |

| latitude | szerokość (ż) | [ʃɛ'rɔkɔɕtʃ] |
| longitude | długość (ż) | ['dwugɔɕtʃ] |
| parallel | równoleżnik (m) | [ruvnɔ'leʒnik] |

| equator | równik (m) | ['ruvnik] |
| sky | niebo (n) | ['nɛbɔ] |
| horizon | horyzont (m) | [hɔ'rizɔnt] |
| atmosphere | atmosfera (ż) | [atmɔs'fɛra] |

| mountain | góra (ż) | ['gura] |
| summit, top | szczyt (m) | [ʃtʃit] |
| cliff | skała (ż) | ['skawa] |
| hill | wzgórze (ż) | ['vzguʒɛ] |

| volcano | wulkan (m) | ['vuʎkan] |
| glacier | lodowiec (m) | [lɔ'dɔvɛts] |
| waterfall | wodospad (m) | [vɔ'dɔspat] |
| plain | równina (ż) | [ruv'nina] |

| river | rzeka (m) | ['ʒɛka] |
| spring (natural source) | źródło (n) | ['ʑrudwɔ] |
| bank (of river) | brzeg (m) | [bʒɛk] |
| downstream (adv) | z prądem | [s 'prɔ̃dɛm] |
| upstream (adv) | pod prąd | [pɔt prɔ̃t] |

| lake | jezioro (m) | [e'ʒɔrɔ] |
| dam | tama (ż) | ['tama] |
| canal | kanał (m) | ['kanaw] |
| swamp (marshland) | bagno (n) | ['bagnɔ] |
| ice | lód (m) | [lyt] |

## 19. Countries of the world. Part 1

| Europe | Europa (ż) | [ɛu'rɔpa] |
| European Union | Unia (ż) Europejska | ['uɲja ɛurɔ'pɛjska] |
| European (n) | Europejczyk (m) | [ɛurɔ'pɛjtʃik] |
| European (adj) | europejski | [ɛurɔ'pɛjski] |

| Austria | Austria (ż) | ['austrʲja] |
| Great Britain | Wielka Brytania (ż) | ['vɛʎka bri'taɲja] |
| England | Anglia (ż) | ['aɲʎja] |
| Belgium | Belgia (ż) | ['bɛʎgʲja] |
| Germany | Niemcy (l.mn.) | ['nemtsi] |

| Netherlands | Niderlandy (l.mn.) | [nidɛr'ʎandi] |
| Holland | Holandia (ż) | [hɔ'ʎandʲja] |
| Greece | Grecja (ż) | ['grɛtsʲja] |
| Denmark | Dania (ż) | ['daɲja] |
| Ireland | Irlandia (ż) | [ir'ʎandʲja] |

| Iceland | Islandia (ż) | [is'ʎandʲja] |
| Spain | Hiszpania (ż) | [hiʃ'paɲja] |
| Italy | Włochy (l.mn.) | ['vwɔhi] |
| Cyprus | Cypr (m) | [tsipr] |

| Malta | Malta (ż) | ['maʎta] |
| Norway | Norwegia (ż) | [nɔr'vɛgʰja] |
| Portugal | Portugalia (ż) | [pɔrtu'gaʎja] |
| Finland | Finlandia (ż) | [fin'ʎandʰja] |
| France | Francja (ż) | ['frantsʰja] |
| Sweden | Szwecja (ż) | ['ʃfɛtsʰja] |

| Switzerland | Szwajcaria (ż) | [ʃfaj'tsarʰja] |
| Scotland | Szkocja (ż) | ['ʃkɔtsʰja] |
| Vatican | Watykan (m) | [va'tikan] |
| Liechtenstein | Liechtenstein (m) | ['lihtɛnʃtajn] |
| Luxembourg | Luksemburg (m) | ['lyksɛmburk] |

| Monaco | Monako (n) | [mɔ'nakɔ] |
| Albania | Albania (ż) | [aʎ'baɲja] |
| Bulgaria | Bułgaria (ż) | [buw'garʰja] |
| Hungary | Węgry (l.mn.) | ['vɛŋri] |
| Latvia | Łotwa (ż) | ['wɔtfa] |

| Lithuania | Litwa (ż) | ['litfa] |
| Poland | Polska (ż) | ['pɔʎska] |
| Romania | Rumunia (ż) | [ru'muɲja] |
| Serbia | Serbia (ż) | ['sɛrbʰja] |
| Slovakia | Słowacja (ż) | [swɔ'vatsʰja] |

| Croatia | Chorwacja (ż) | [hɔr'vatsʰja] |
| Czech Republic | Czechy (l.mn.) | ['tʃɛhi] |
| Estonia | Estonia (ż) | [ɛs'tɔɲja] |
| Bosnia and Herzegovina | Bośnia i Hercegowina (ż) | ['bɔɕɲa i hɛrtsɛgɔ'vina] |
| Macedonia (Republic of ~) | Macedonia (ż) | [matsɛ'dɔɲja] |

| Slovenia | Słowenia (ż) | [swɔ'vɛɲja] |
| Montenegro | Czarnogóra (ż) | [tʃarnɔ'gura] |
| Belarus | Białoruś (ż) | [bʲa'wɔruɕ] |
| Moldova, Moldavia | Mołdawia (ż) | [mɔw'davʰja] |
| Russia | Rosja (ż) | ['rɔsʰja] |
| Ukraine | Ukraina (ż) | [ukra'ina] |

## 20. Countries of the world. Part 2

| Asia | Azja (ż) | ['azʰja] |
| Vietnam | Wietnam (m) | ['vʰetnam] |
| India | Indie (l.mn.) | ['indʰe] |
| Israel | Izrael (m) | [iz'raɛʎ] |
| China | Chiny (l.mn.) | ['hinɨ] |

| Lebanon | Liban (m) | ['liban] |
| Mongolia | Mongolia (ż) | [mɔ'ŋɔʎja] |
| Malaysia | Malezja (ż) | [ma'lezʰja] |
| Pakistan | Pakistan (m) | [pa'kistan] |

| | | |
|---|---|---|
| Saudi Arabia | **Arabia** (ż) **Saudyjska** | [a'rabʰja sau'dijska] |
| Thailand | **Tajlandia** (ż) | [taj'ʎandʰja] |
| Taiwan | **Tajwan** (m) | ['tajvan] |
| Turkey | **Turcja** (ż) | ['turʦʰja] |
| Japan | **Japonia** (ż) | [ja'pɔɲja] |
| Afghanistan | **Afganistan** (n) | [avga'nistan] |
| | | |
| Bangladesh | **Bangladesz** (m) | [baŋʎa'dɛʃ] |
| Indonesia | **Indonezja** (ż) | [indɔ'nɛzʰja] |
| Jordan | **Jordania** (ż) | [ʒr'daɲja] |
| Iraq | **Irak** (m) | ['irak] |
| Iran | **Iran** (m) | ['iran] |
| | | |
| Cambodia | **Kambodża** (ż) | [kam'bɔʤa] |
| Kuwait | **Kuwejt** (m) | ['kuvɛjt] |
| Laos | **Laos** (m) | ['ʎaɔs] |
| Myanmar | **Mjanma** (ż) | ['mjanma] |
| Nepal | **Nepal** (m) | ['nɛpaʎ] |
| | | |
| United Arab Emirates | **Zjednoczone Emiraty Arabskie** | [zʰednɔt'ʃɔnɛ ɛmi'rati a'rapske] |
| Syria | **Syria** (ż) | ['siɾʰja] |
| Palestine | **Autonomia** (ż) **Palestyńska** | [autɔ'nɔmʰja pales'tiɲska] |
| South Korea | **Korea** (ż) **Południowa** | [kɔ'rɛa pɔwud'nʒva] |
| North Korea | **Korea** (ż) **Północna** | [kɔ'rɛa puw'nɔʦna] |
| | | |
| United States of America | **Stany** (l.mn.) **Zjednoczone Ameryki** | ['stani zʰednɔt'ʃɔnɛ a'mɛriki] |
| Canada | **Kanada** (ż) | [ka'nada] |
| Mexico | **Meksyk** (m) | ['mɛksɨk] |
| Argentina | **Argentyna** (ż) | [argɛn'tina] |
| Brazil | **Brazylia** (ż) | [bra'ziʎja] |
| | | |
| Colombia | **Kolumbia** (ż) | [kɔ'lymbʰja] |
| Cuba | **Kuba** (ż) | ['kuba] |
| Chile | **Chile** (n) | ['ʧile] |
| Venezuela | **Wenezuela** (ż) | [vɛnɛzu'ɛʎa] |
| Ecuador | **Ekwador** (m) | [ɛk'fadɔr] |
| | | |
| The Bahamas | **Wyspy** (l.mn.) **Bahama** | ['vispɨ ba'hama] |
| Panama | **Panama** (ż) | [pa'nama] |
| Egypt | **Egipt** (m) | ['ɛgipt] |
| | | |
| Morocco | **Maroko** (n) | [ma'rɔkɔ] |
| Tunisia | **Tunezja** (ż) | [tu'nɛzʰja] |
| | | |
| Kenya | **Kenia** (ż) | ['kɛɲja] |
| Libya | **Libia** (ż) | ['libʰja] |
| South Africa | **Afryka** (ż) **Południowa** | ['afrika pɔwud'nʒva] |
| Australia | **Australia** (ż) | [aust'raʎja] |
| New Zealand | **Nowa Zelandia** (ż) | ['nɔva zɛ'ʎandʰja] |

## 21. Weather. Natural disasters

| weather | pogoda (ż) | [pɔ'gɔda] |
| weather forecast | prognoza (ż) pogody | [prɔg'nɔza pɔ'gɔdɨ] |
| temperature | temperatura (ż) | [tɛmpɛra'tura] |
| thermometer | termometr (m) | [tɛr'mɔmɛtr] |
| barometer | barometr (m) | [ba'rɔmɛtr] |

| sun | słońce (n) | ['swɔɲtsɛ] |
| to shine (vi) | świecić | ['ɕfetʃitʃ] |
| sunny (day) | słoneczny | [swɔ'nɛtʃnɨ] |
| to come up (vi) | wzejść | [vzɛjɕtʃ] |
| to set (vi) | zajść | [zajɕtʃ] |

| rain | deszcz (m) | [dɛʃtʃ] |
| it's raining | pada deszcz | ['pada dɛʃtʃ] |
| pouring rain | ulewny deszcz (m) | [u'levnɨ dɛʃtʃ] |
| rain cloud | chmura (ż) | ['hmura] |
| puddle | kałuża (ż) | [ka'wuʒa] |
| to get wet (in rain) | moknąć | ['mɔknɔ̃tʃ] |

| thunderstorm | burza (ż) | ['buʒa] |
| lightning (~ strike) | błyskawica (ż) | [bwɨska'vitsa] |
| to flash (vi) | błyskać | ['bwɨskatʃ] |
| thunder | grzmot (m) | [gʒmɔt] |
| it's thundering | grzmi | [gʒmi] |
| hail | grad (m) | [grat] |
| it's hailing | pada grad | ['pada grat] |

| heat (extreme ~) | żar (m) | [ʒar] |
| it's hot | gorąco | [gɔ'rɔ̃tsɔ] |
| it's warm | ciepło | ['tʃepwɔ] |
| it's cold | zimno | ['ʒimnɔ] |

| fog (mist) | mgła (ż) | [mgwa] |
| foggy | mglisty | ['mglistɨ] |
| cloud | obłok (m) | ['ɔbwɔk] |
| cloudy (adj) | zachmurzony | [zahmu'ʒɔnɨ] |
| humidity | wilgoć (ż) | ['viʎgɔtʃ] |

| snow | śnieg (m) | [ɕnek] |
| it's snowing | pada śnieg | ['pada ɕnek] |
| frost (severe ~, freezing cold) | mróz (m) | [mrus] |
| below zero (adv) | poniżej zera | [pɔ'niʒɛj 'zɛra] |
| hoarfrost | szron (m) | [ʃrɔn] |

| bad weather | niepogoda (ż) | [nepɔ'gɔda] |
| disaster | katastrofa (ż) | [katast'rɔfa] |
| flood, inundation | powódź (ż) | ['pɔvutʃ] |
| avalanche | lawina (ż) | [ʎa'vina] |

| earthquake | trzęsienie (n) ziemi | [tʃɛ̃'ɕene 'ʒemi] |
| tremor, quake | wstrząs (m) | [fstʃɔ̃s] |
| epicenter | epicentrum (n) | [ɛpi'tsɛntrum] |
| eruption | wybuch (m) | ['vɨbuh] |
| lava | lawa (z) | ['ʎava] |

| tornado | tornado (n) | [tɔr'nadɔ] |
| twister | trąba (z) powietrzna | ['trɔ̃ba pɔ'vetʃna] |
| hurricane | huragan (m) | [hu'ragan] |
| tsunami | tsunami (n) | [ʦu'nami] |
| cyclone | cyklon (m) | ['ʦiklɜn] |

## 22. Animals. Part 1

| animal | zwierzę (n) | ['zveʒɛ̃] |
| predator | drapieżnik (m) | [dra'peʒnik] |

| tiger | tygrys (m) | ['tɨgris] |
| lion | lew (m) | [lef] |
| wolf | wilk (m) | [viʎk] |
| fox | lis (m) | [lis] |
| jaguar | jaguar (m) | [ja'guar] |

| lynx | ryś (m) | [riɕ] |
| coyote | kojot (m) | ['kɔɔt] |
| jackal | szakal (m) | ['ʃakaʎ] |
| hyena | hiena (z) | ['hʰena] |

| squirrel | wiewiórka (z) | [ve'vyrka] |
| hedgehog | jeż (m) | [eʃ] |
| rabbit | królik (m) | ['krulik] |
| raccoon | szop (m) | [ʃɔp] |

| hamster | chomik (m) | ['hɔmik] |
| mole | kret (m) | [krɛt] |
| mouse | mysz (z) | [miʃ] |
| rat | szczur (m) | [ʃtʃur] |
| bat | nietoperz (m) | [ne'tɔpɛʃ] |

| beaver | bóbr (m) | [bubr] |
| horse | koń (m) | [kɔɲ] |
| deer | jeleń (m) | ['eleɲ] |
| camel | wielbłąd (m) | ['veʎbwɔ̃t] |
| zebra | zebra (z) | ['zɛbra] |

| whale | wieloryb (m) | [ve'lɜrip] |
| seal | foka (z) | ['fɔka] |
| walrus | mors (m) | [mɔrs] |
| dolphin | delfin (m) | ['dɛʎfin] |
| bear | niedźwiedź (m) | ['nedʑʲvetʃ] |

| monkey | **małpa** (ż) | ['mawpa] |
| elephant | **słoń** (m) | ['swɔɲ] |
| rhinoceros | **nosorożec** (m) | [nɔsɔ'rɔʒɛts] |
| giraffe | **żyrafa** (ż) | [ʒi'rafa] |

| hippopotamus | **hipopotam** (m) | [hipɔ'pɔtam] |
| kangaroo | **kangur** (m) | ['kaŋur] |
| cat | **kotka** (ż) | ['kɔtka] |
| dog | **pies** (m) | [pes] |

| cow | **krowa** (ż) | ['krɔva] |
| bull | **byk** (m) | [bɨk] |
| sheep (ewe) | **owca** (ż) | ['ɔftsa] |
| goat | **koza** (ż) | ['kɔza] |

| donkey | **osioł** (m) | ['ɔɕɔw] |
| pig, hog | **świnia** (ż) | ['ɕfiɲa] |
| hen (chicken) | **kura** (ż) | ['kura] |
| rooster | **kogut** (m) | ['kɔgut] |

| duck | **kaczka** (ż) | ['katʃka] |
| goose | **gęś** (ż) | [gɛ̃ɕ] |
| turkey (hen) | **indyczka** (ż) | [in'dɨtʃka] |
| sheepdog | **owczarek** (m) | [ɔft'ʃarɛk] |

## 23. Animals. Part 2

| bird | **ptak** (m) | [ptak] |
| pigeon | **gołąb** (m) | ['gɔwɔ̃p] |
| sparrow | **wróbel** (m) | ['vrubɛʎ] |
| tit | **sikorka** (ż) | [ɕi'kɔrka] |
| magpie | **sroka** (ż) | ['srɔka] |

| eagle | **orzeł** (m) | ['ɔʒɛw] |
| hawk | **jastrząb** (m) | ['jastʃɔ̃p] |
| falcon | **sokół** (m) | ['sɔkuw] |

| swan | **łabędź** (m) | ['wabɛ̃tʃ] |
| crane | **żuraw** (m) | ['ʒuraf] |
| stork | **bocian** (m) | ['bɔtɕan] |
| parrot | **papuga** (ż) | [pa'puga] |
| peacock | **paw** (m) | [paf] |
| ostrich | **struś** (m) | [struɕ] |

| heron | **czapla** (ż) | ['tʃapʎa] |
| nightingale | **słowik** (m) | ['swɔvik] |
| swallow | **jaskółka** (ż) | [jas'kuwka] |
| woodpecker | **dzięcioł** (m) | ['dʒɛ̃tɕɔw] |
| cuckoo | **kukułka** (ż) | [ku'kuwka] |
| owl | **sowa** (ż) | ['sɔva] |

| penguin | pingwin (m) | ['piŋvin] |
| tuna | tuńczyk (m) | ['tuntʃik] |
| trout | pstrąg (m) | [pstrɔ̃k] |
| eel | węgorz (m) | ['vɛŋɔʃ] |

| shark | rekin (m) | ['rɛkin] |
| crab | krab (m) | [krap] |
| jellyfish | meduza (ż) | [mɛ'duza] |
| octopus | ośmiornica (ż) | [ɔɕmɔr'niʦa] |

| starfish | rozgwiazda (ż) | [rɔzg'vʲazda] |
| sea urchin | jeżowiec (m) | [e'ʒɔveʦ] |
| seahorse | konik (m) morski | ['kɔnik 'mɔrski] |
| shrimp | krewetka (ż) | [krɛ'vɛtka] |

| snake | wąż (m) | [vɔ̃ʃ] |
| viper | żmija (ż) | ['ʒmija] |
| lizard | jaszczurka (ż) | [jaʃt'ʃurka] |
| iguana | legwan (m) | ['legvan] |
| chameleon | kameleon (m) | [kamɛ'leɔn] |
| scorpion | skorpion (m) | ['skɔrpʰɔn] |

| turtle | żółw (m) | [ʒuwf] |
| frog | żaba (ż) | ['ʒaba] |
| crocodile | krokodyl (m) | [krɔ'kɔdiʎ] |

| insect, bug | owad (m) | ['ɔvat] |
| butterfly | motyl (m) | ['mɔtiʎ] |
| ant | mrówka (ż) | ['mrufka] |
| fly | mucha (ż) | ['muha] |

| mosquito | komar (m) | ['kɔmar] |
| beetle | żuk (m), chrząszcz (m) | [ʒuk], [hʃɔ̃ʃtʃ] |
| bee | pszczoła (ż) | ['pʃtʃɔwa] |
| spider | pająk (m) | ['paɔ̃k] |

## 24. Trees. Plants

| tree | drzewo (n) | ['dʒɛvɔ] |
| birch | brzoza (ż) | ['bʒɔza] |
| oak | dąb (m) | [dɔ̃p] |
| linden tree | lipa (ż) | ['lipa] |
| aspen | osika (ż) | [ɔ'ɕika] |

| maple | klon (m) | ['klɔn] |
| spruce | świerk (m) | ['ɕferk] |
| pine | sosna (ż) | ['sɔsna] |
| cedar | cedr (m) | [ʦɛdr] |
| poplar | topola (ż) | [tɔ'pɔʎa] |
| rowan | jarzębina (ż) | [jaʒɛ̃'bina] |

| | | |
|---|---|---|
| beech | **buk** (m) | [buk] |
| elm | **wiąz** (m) | [võz] |
| ash (tree) | **jesion** (m) | ['eɕɜn] |
| chestnut | **kasztan** (m) | ['kaʃtan] |
| palm tree | **palma** (ż) | ['paʎma] |
| bush | **krzew** (m) | [kʃɛf] |

| | | |
|---|---|---|
| mushroom | **grzyb** (m) | [gʒɨp] |
| poisonous mushroom | **grzyb** (m) **trujący** | [gʒɨp truɔ̃tɕi] |
| cep (Boletus edulis) | **prawdziwek** (m) | [prav'dʒivɛk] |
| russula | **gołąbek** (m) | [gɔ'wõbɛk] |
| fly agaric | **muchomor** (m) | [mu'hɔmɔr] |
| death cap | **psi grzyb** (m) | [pɕi gʒɨp] |

| | | |
|---|---|---|
| flower | **kwiat** (m) | [kfʲat] |
| bouquet (of flowers) | **bukiet** (m) | ['buket] |
| rose (flower) | **róża** (ż) | ['ruʒa] |
| tulip | **tulipan** (m) | [tu'lipan] |
| carnation | **goździk** (m) | ['gɔʑʲdʒik] |

| | | |
|---|---|---|
| camomile | **rumianek** (m) | [ru'mʲanɛk] |
| cactus | **kaktus** (m) | ['kaktus] |
| lily of the valley | **konwalia** (ż) | [kɔn'vaʎja] |
| snowdrop | **przebiśnieg** (m) | [pʃɛ'biɕnek] |
| water lily | **lilia wodna** (ż) | ['liʎja 'vɔdna] |

| | | |
|---|---|---|
| greenhouse (tropical ~) | **szklarnia** (ż) | ['ʃkʎarɲa] |
| lawn | **trawnik** (m) | ['travnik] |
| flowerbed | **klomb** (m) | ['klɜmp] |

| | | |
|---|---|---|
| plant | **roślina** (ż) | [rɔɕ'lina] |
| grass | **trawa** (ż) | ['trava] |
| leaf | **liść** (m) | [liɕtʃ] |
| petal | **płatek** (m) | ['pwatɛk] |
| stem | **łodyga** (ż) | [wɔ'diga] |
| young plant (shoot) | **kiełek** (m) | ['kewɛk] |

| | | |
|---|---|---|
| cereal crops | **zboża** (l.mn.) | ['zbɔʒa] |
| wheat | **pszenica** (ż) | [pʃɛ'nitsa] |
| rye | **żyto** (n) | ['ʒitɔ] |
| oats | **owies** (m) | ['ɔves] |
| millet | **proso** (n) | ['prɔsɔ] |
| barley | **jęczmień** (m) | ['entʃmɛ̃] |
| corn | **kukurydza** (ż) | [kuku'ridza] |
| rice | **ryż** (m) | [riʃ] |

## 25. Various useful words

| | | |
|---|---|---|
| balance (of situation) | **równowaga** (ż) | [ruvnɔ'vaga] |
| base (basis) | **baza** (ż) | ['baza] |

| | | |
|---|---|---|
| beginning | **początek** (m) | [pɔt'ʃɔtɛk] |
| category | **kategoria** (ż) | [katɛ'gɔrʰja] |
| | | |
| choice | **wybór** (m) | ['vɨbur] |
| coincidence | **koincydencja** (ż) | [kɔjnsɨ'dɛnsija] |
| comparison | **porównanie** (n) | [pɔruv'nane] |
| degree (extent, amount) | **stopień** (m) | ['stɔpeɲ] |
| | | |
| development | **rozwój** (m) | ['rɔzvuj] |
| difference | **różnica** (ż) | [ruʒ'nitsa] |
| effect (e.g., of drugs) | **efekt** (m) | ['ɛfɛkt] |
| effort (exertion) | **wysiłek** (m) | [vɨ'ɕiwɛk] |
| | | |
| element | **element** (m) | [ɛ'lemɛnt] |
| example (illustration) | **przykład** (m) | ['pʃɨkwat] |
| fact | **fakt** (m) | [fakt] |
| help | **pomoc** (ż) | ['pɔmɔts] |
| | | |
| ideal | **ideał** (m) | [i'dɛaw] |
| kind (sort, type) | **rodzaj** (m) | ['rɔdzaj] |
| mistake, error | **błąd** (m) | [bwɔ̃t] |
| moment | **moment** (m) | ['mɔmɛnt] |
| | | |
| obstacle | **przeszkoda** (ż) | [pʃɛʃ'kɔda] |
| part (~ of sth) | **część** (ż) | [tʃɛ̃ɕtʃ] |
| pause (break) | **pauza** (ż) | ['pauza] |
| position | **stanowisko** (n) | [stanɔ'viskɔ] |
| | | |
| problem | **problem** (m) | ['prɔblem] |
| process | **proces** (m) | ['prɔtsɛs] |
| progress | **postęp** (m) | ['pɔstɛ̃p] |
| property (quality) | **właściwość** (ż) | [vwaɕ'tʃivɔɕtʃ] |
| | | |
| reaction | **reakcja** (ż) | [rɛ'aktsʰja] |
| risk | **ryzyko** (n) | ['rizɨkɔ] |
| secret | **tajemnica** (ż) | [taem'nitsa] |
| series | **seria** (ż) | ['sɛrʰja] |
| | | |
| shape (outer form) | **kształt** (m) | ['kʃtawt] |
| situation | **sytuacja** (ż) | [sɨtu'atsʰja] |
| solution | **rozwiązanie** (n) | [rɔzvɔ̃'zane] |
| standard (adj) | **standardowy** | [standar'dɔvi] |
| | | |
| stop (pause) | **przerwa** (ż) | ['pʃɛrva] |
| style | **styl** (m) | [stiʎ] |
| system | **system** (m) | ['sistɛm] |
| table (chart) | **tablica** (ż) | [tab'litsa] |
| tempo, rate | **tempo** (n) | ['tɛmpɔ] |
| | | |
| term (word, expression) | **termin** (m) | ['tɛrmin] |
| truth (e.g., moment of ~) | **prawda** (ż) | ['pravda] |

| turn (please wait your ~) | kolej (ż) | ['kɔlej] |
| urgent (adj) | pilny | ['piʎɲi] |

| utility (usefulness) | korzyść (ż) | ['kɔʑiɕt͡ʂ] |
| variant (alternative) | wariant (m) | ['varʲjant] |
| way (means, method) | sposób (m) | ['spɔsup] |
| zone | strefa (ż) | ['strɛfa] |

## 26. Modifiers. Adjectives. Part 1

| additional (adj) | dodatkowy | [dɔdat'kɔvi] |
| ancient (~ civilization) | dawny | ['davni] |
| artificial (adj) | sztuczny | ['ʃtut͡ʃɲi] |
| bad (adj) | zły | [zwi] |
| beautiful (person) | piękny | ['peŋkɲi] |

| big (in size) | duży | ['duʒi] |
| bitter (taste) | gorzki | ['gɔʃki] |
| blind (sightless) | ślepy | ['ɕlepi] |
| central (adj) | centralny | [t͡sɛnt'raʎɲi] |

| children's (adj) | dziecięcy | [d͡ʑe't͡ʃɛɲt͡si] |
| clandestine (secret) | podziemny | [pɔ'd͡ʑemɲi] |
| clean (free from dirt) | czysty | ['t͡ʃisti] |
| clever (smart) | sprytny | ['spritɲi] |
| compatible (adj) | kompatybilny | [kɔmpati'biʎɲi] |

| contented (satisfied) | zadowolony | [zadɔvɔ'lɔɲi] |
| dangerous (adj) | niebezpieczny | [nebɛs'pet͡ʃɲi] |
| dead (not alive) | martwy | ['martfi] |
| dense (fog, smoke) | gęsty | ['gɛnsti] |
| difficult (decision) | trudny | ['trudɲi] |

| dirty (not clean) | brudny | ['brudɲi] |
| easy (not difficult) | łatwy | ['watfi] |
| empty (glass, room) | pusty | ['pusti] |
| exact (amount) | dokładny | [dɔk'wadɲi] |
| excellent (adj) | świetny | ['ɕfetɲi] |

| excessive (adj) | nadmierny | [nad'merɲi] |
| exterior (adj) | zewnętrzny | [zɛv'nɛnt͡ʃɲi] |
| fast (quick) | szybki | ['ʃipki] |
| fertile (land, soil) | urodzajny | [urɔ'd͡zajɲi] |
| fragile (china, glass) | kruchy | ['kruhi] |

| free (at no cost) | bezpłatny | [bɛsp'watɲi] |
| fresh (~ water) | słodki | ['swɔtki] |
| frozen (food) | mrożony | [mrɔ'ʒɔɲi] |
| full (completely filled) | pełny | ['pɛwɲi] |
| happy (adj) | szczęśliwy | [ʃt͡ʃɛ̃ɕ'livi] |

| hard (not soft) | twardy | ['tfardɨ] |
|---|---|---|
| huge (adj) | ogromny | [ɔg'rɔmnɨ] |
| ill (sick, unwell) | chory | ['hɔrɨ] |
| immobile (adj) | nieruchomy | [neru'hɔmɨ] |
| important (adj) | ważny | ['vaʒnɨ] |

| interior (adj) | wewnętrzny | [vɛv'nɛntʃnɨ] |
|---|---|---|
| last (e.g., ~ week) | ubiegły | [u'begwɨ] |
| last (final) | ostatni | [ɔs'tatni] |
| left (e.g., ~ side) | lewy | ['levɨ] |
| legal (legitimate) | prawny | ['pravnɨ] |

| light (in weight) | lekki | ['lekki] |
|---|---|---|
| liquid (fluid) | płynny | ['pwɨɲɨ] |
| long (e.g., ~ hair) | długi | ['dwugi] |
| loud (voice, etc.) | głośny | ['gwɔɕnɨ] |
| low (voice) | cichy | ['tʃihɨ] |

## 27. Modifiers. Adjectives. Part 2

| main (principal) | główny | ['gwuvnɨ] |
|---|---|---|
| matt, matte | matowy | [ma'tɔvɨ] |
| mysterious (adj) | tajemniczy | [taem'nitʃɨ] |
| narrow (street, etc.) | wąski | ['võski] |
| native (~ country) | ojczysty | [ɔjt'ʃistɨ] |

| negative (~ response) | negatywny | [nɛga'tivnɨ] |
|---|---|---|
| new (adj) | nowy | ['nɔvɨ] |
| next (e.g., ~ week) | następny | [nas'tɛ̃pnɨ] |
| normal (adj) | normalny | [nɔr'maʎnɨ] |
| not difficult (adj) | nietrudny | [net'rudnɨ] |

| obligatory (adj) | obowiązkowy | [ɔbɔvʲɔ̃s'kɔvɨ] |
|---|---|---|
| old (house) | stary | ['starɨ] |
| open (adj) | otwarty | [ɔt'fartɨ] |
| opposite (adj) | przeciwny | [pʃɛ'tʃivnɨ] |
| ordinary (usual) | zwykły | ['zvɨkwɨ] |

| original (unusual) | oryginalny | [ɔrigi'naʎnɨ] |
|---|---|---|
| personal (adj) | osobisty | [ɔsɔ'bistɨ] |
| polite (adj) | uprzejmy | [up'ʃɛjmɨ] |
| poor (not rich) | biedny | ['bednɨ] |

| possible (adj) | możliwy | [mɔʒ'livɨ] |
|---|---|---|
| principal (main) | podstawowy | [pɔtsta'vɔvɨ] |
| probable (adj) | prawdopodobny | [pravdɔpɔ'dɔbnɨ] |
| prolonged (e.g., ~ applause) | długotrwały | [dwugɔtr'fawɨ] |
| public (open to all) | publiczny | [pub'litʃnɨ] |
| rare (adj) | rzadki | ['ʒatki] |

| | | |
|---|---|---|
| raw (uncooked) | **surowy** | [su'rɔvɨ] |
| right (not left) | **prawy** | ['pravɨ] |
| ripe (fruit) | **dojrzały** | [dɔj'ʒawɨ] |

| | | |
|---|---|---|
| risky (adj) | **ryzykowny** | [rizi'kɔvnɨ] |
| sad (~ look) | **smutny** | ['smutnɨ] |
| second hand (adj) | **używany** | [uʒɨ'vanɨ] |
| shallow (water) | **płytki** | ['pwitki] |
| sharp (blade, etc.) | **ostry** | ['ɔstrɨ] |

| | | |
|---|---|---|
| short (in length) | **krótki** | ['krutki] |
| similar (adj) | **podobny** | [pɔ'dɔbnɨ] |
| small (in size) | **mały** | ['mawɨ] |
| smooth (surface) | **gładki** | ['gwatki] |
| soft (~ toys) | **miękki** | ['menki] |

| | | |
|---|---|---|
| solid (~ wall) | **trwały** | ['trfawɨ] |
| sour (flavor, taste) | **kwaśny** | ['kfaɕnɨ] |
| spacious (house, etc.) | **przestronny** | [pʃɛst'rɔɲɨ] |
| special (adj) | **specjalny** | [spɛts̪ʲ'jaʎɨ] |

| | | |
|---|---|---|
| straight (line, road) | **prosty** | ['prɔsti] |
| strong (person) | **silny** | ['ɕiʎɨ] |
| stupid (foolish) | **głupi** | ['gwupi] |
| superb, perfect (adj) | **doskonały** | [dɔskɔ'nawɨ] |

| | | |
|---|---|---|
| sweet (sugary) | **słodki** | ['swɔtki] |
| tan (adj) | **opalony** | [ɔpa'lɔnɨ] |
| tasty (delicious) | **smaczny** | ['smatʃnɨ] |
| unclear (adj) | **niejasny** | [ne'jasnɨ] |

## 28. Verbs. Part 1

| | | |
|---|---|---|
| to accuse (vt) | **obwiniać** | [ɔb'viɲatʃ] |
| to agree (say yes) | **zgadzać się** | ['zgadzatʃ ɕɛ̃] |
| to announce (vt) | **ogłaszać** | [ɔg'waʃatʃ] |
| to answer (vi, vt) | **odpowiadać** | [ɔtpɔ'vʲadatʃ] |
| to apologize (vi) | **przepraszać** | [pʃɛp'raʃatʃ] |

| | | |
|---|---|---|
| to arrive (vi) | **przyjeżdżać** | [pʃɨ'eʒdʒatʃ] |
| to ask (~ oneself) | **pytać** | ['pitatʃ] |
| to be absent | **być nieobecnym** | [bitʃ neɔ'bɛtsnim] |
| to be afraid | **bać się** | [batʃ ɕɛ̃] |
| to be born | **urodzić się** | [u'rɔdʑitʃ ɕɛ̃] |

| | | |
|---|---|---|
| to be in a hurry | **śpieszyć się** | ['ɕpeʃitʃ ɕɛ̃] |
| to beat (to hit) | **bić** | [bitʃ] |
| to begin (vt) | **rozpoczynać** | [rɔspɔt'ʃɨnatʃ] |
| to believe (in God) | **wierzyć** | ['veʒitʃ] |
| to belong to ... | **należeć** | [na'leʒɛtʃ] |

| | | |
|---|---|---|
| to break (split into pieces) | psuć | [psutʃ] |
| to build (vt) | budować | [buˈdɔvatʃ] |
| to buy (purchase) | kupować | [kuˈpɔvatʃ] |
| can (v aux) | móc | [muts] |
| can (v aux) | móc | [muts] |
| to cancel (call off) | odwołać | [ɔdˈvɔwatʃ] |
| | | |
| to catch (vt) | łowić | [ˈwɔvitʃ] |
| to change (vt) | zmienić | [ˈzmenitʃ] |
| to check (to examine) | sprawdzać | [ˈspravdzatʃ] |
| to choose (select) | wybierać | [viˈberatʃ] |
| to clean up (tidy) | sprzątać | [ˈspʃɔtatʃ] |
| | | |
| to close (vt) | zamykać | [zaˈmɨkatʃ] |
| to compare (vt) | porównywać | [pɔruvˈnɨvatʃ] |
| to complain (vi, vt) | skarżyć się | [ˈskarʒitʃ ɕɛ̃] |
| to confirm (vt) | potwierdzić | [pɔtˈferdʒitʃ] |
| to congratulate (vt) | gratulować | [gratuˈlɔvatʃ] |
| | | |
| to cook (dinner) | gotować | [gɔˈtɔvatʃ] |
| to copy (vt) | skopiować | [skɔˈpʲɔvatʃ] |
| to cost (vt) | kosztować | [kɔʃˈtɔvatʃ] |
| to count (add up) | liczyć | [ˈlitʃitʃ] |
| to count on ... | liczyć na ... | [ˈlitʃitʃ na] |
| | | |
| to create (vt) | stworzyć | [ˈstfɔʒitʃ] |
| to cry (weep) | płakać | [ˈpwakatʃ] |
| to dance (vi, vt) | tańczyć | [ˈtaɲtʃitʃ] |
| to deceive (vi, vt) | oszukiwać | [ɔʃuˈkivatʃ] |
| to decide (~ to do sth) | decydować | [dɛtsiˈdɔvatʃ] |
| | | |
| to delete (vt) | usunąć | [uˈsunɔ̃tʃ] |
| to demand (request firmly) | zażądać | [zaˈʒɔ̃datʃ] |
| to deny (vt) | zaprzeczać | [zapˈʃɛtʃatʃ] |
| to depend on ... | zależeć od ... | [zaˈlɛʒɛtʃ ɔd] |
| to despise (vt) | pogardzać | [pɔˈgardzatʃ] |
| | | |
| to die (vi) | umrzeć | [ˈumʒɛtʃ] |
| to dig (vt) | kopać | [ˈkɔpatʃ] |
| to disappear (vi) | zniknąć | [ˈzniknɔ̃tʃ] |
| to discuss (vt) | omawiać | [ɔˈmavʲatʃ] |
| to disturb (vt) | przeszkadzać | [pʃɛʃˈkadzatʃ] |

## 29. Verbs. Part 2

| | | |
|---|---|---|
| to dive (vi) | nurkować | [nurˈkɔvatʃ] |
| to divorce (vi) | rozwieść się | [ˈrɔzvɛɕtʃ ɕɛ̃] |
| to do (vt) | robić | [ˈrɔbitʃ] |
| to doubt (have doubts) | wątpić | [ˈvɔ̃tpitʃ] |
| to drink (vi, vt) | pić | [pitʃ] |

| | | |
|---|---|---|
| to drop (let fall) | **upuszczać** | [u'puʃʧatʃ] |
| to dry (clothes, hair) | **suszyć** | ['suʃiʧ] |
| to eat (vi, vt) | **jeść** | [eɕʧ] |
| to end (~ a relationship) | **zakończyć** | [za'kɔnʧiʧ] |
| to excuse (forgive) | **wybaczać** | [vi'baʧaʧ] |
| | | |
| to exist (vi) | **istnieć** | ['istneʧ] |
| to expect (foresee) | **przewidzieć** | [pʃɛ'vidʒeʧ] |
| to explain (vt) | **objaśniać** | [ɔbʰ'jaɕnaʧ] |
| to fall (vi) | **spadać** | ['spadaʧ] |
| to fight (street fight, etc.) | **bić się** | [biʧ ɕɛ̃] |
| to find (vt) | **znajdować** | [znaj'dɔvaʧ] |
| | | |
| to finish (vt) | **kończyć** | ['kɔnʧiʧ] |
| to fly (vi) | **lecieć** | ['leʧeʧ] |
| to forbid (vt) | **zakazać** | [za'kazaʧ] |
| to forget (vi, vt) | **zapominać** | [zapɔ'minaʧ] |
| to forgive (vt) | **przebaczać** | [pʃɛ'baʧaʧ] |
| | | |
| to get tired | **być zmęczonym** | [biʧ zmɛ̃'ʧɔnim] |
| to give (vt) | **dawać** | ['davaʧ] |
| to go (on foot) | **iść** | [iɕʧ] |
| to hate (vt) | **nienawidzieć** | [nena'vidʒeʧ] |
| to have (vt) | **mieć** | [meʧ] |
| to have breakfast | **jeść śniadanie** | [eɕʧ ɕɲa'dane] |
| to have dinner | **jeść kolację** | [eɕʧ kɔ'ʌatsʰɛ̃] |
| to have lunch | **jeść obiad** | [eɕʧ 'ɔbʲat] |
| | | |
| to hear (vt) | **słyszeć** | ['swiʃɛʧ] |
| to help (vt) | **pomagać** | [pɔ'magaʧ] |
| to hide (vt) | **chować** | ['hɔvaʧ] |
| to hope (vi, vt) | **mieć nadzieję** | [meʧ na'dʒeɛ̃] |
| to hunt (vi, vt) | **polować** | [pɔ'lɔvaʧ] |
| to hurry (vi) | **śpieszyć się** | ['ɕpeʃiʧ ɕɛ̃] |
| | | |
| to insist (vi, vt) | **nalegać** | [na'legaʧ] |
| to insult (vt) | **znieważać** | [zne'vaʒaʧ] |
| to invite (vt) | **zapraszać** | [zap'raʃaʧ] |
| to joke (vi) | **żartować** | [ʒar'tɔvaʧ] |
| to keep (vt) | **zachowywać** | [zahɔ'vivaʧ] |
| | | |
| to kill (vt) | **zabijać** | [za'bijaʧ] |
| to know (sb) | **znać** | [znaʧ] |
| to know (sth) | **wiedzieć** | ['vedʒeʧ] |
| to like (I like ...) | **podobać się** | [pɔ'dɔbaʧ ɕɛ̃] |
| to look at ... | **patrzeć** | ['paʧɛʧ] |
| | | |
| to lose (umbrella, etc.) | **tracić** | ['traʧiʧ] |
| to love (sb) | **kochać** | ['kɔhaʧ] |
| to make a mistake | **mylić się** | ['miliʧ ɕɛ̃] |
| to meet (vi, vt) | **spotkać się** | ['spotkaʧ ɕɛ̃] |
| to miss (school, etc.) | **opuszczać** | [ɔ'puʃʧaʧ] |

## 30. Verbs. Part 3

| | | |
|---|---|---|
| to obey (vi, vt) | podporządkować się | [pɔtpɔʒɔd'kɔvatʃ ɕɛ̃] |
| to open (vt) | otwierać | [ɔt'feratʃ] |
| to participate (vi) | uczestniczyć | [utʃɛst'nitʃitʃ] |
| to pay (vi, vt) | płacić | ['pwatʃitʃ] |
| to permit (vt) | zezwalać | [zɛz'vaʎatʃ] |
| | | |
| to play (children) | grać | [gratʃ] |
| to pray (vi, vt) | modlić się | ['mɔdlitʃ ɕɛ̃] |
| to promise (vt) | obiecać | [ɔ'betsatʃ] |
| to propose (vt) | proponować | [prɔpɔ'nɔvatʃ] |
| to prove (vt) | udowadniać | [udɔ'vadɲatʃ] |
| to read (vi, vt) | czytać | ['tʃitatʃ] |
| | | |
| to receive (vt) | odebrać | [ɔ'dɛbratʃ] |
| to rent (sth from sb) | wynajmować | [vinaj'mɔvatʃ] |
| to repeat (say again) | powtarzać | [pɔf'taʒatʃ] |
| to reserve, to book | rezerwować | [rɛzɛr'vɔvatʃ] |
| to run (vi) | biec | [bets] |
| | | |
| to save (rescue) | ratować | [ra'tɔvatʃ] |
| to say (~ thank you) | powiedzieć | [pɔ'vedʒetʃ] |
| to see (vt) | widzieć | ['vidʒetʃ] |
| to sell (vt) | sprzedawać | [spʃɛ'davatʃ] |
| to send (vt) | wysyłać | [vi'siwatʃ] |
| to shoot (vi) | strzelać | ['stʃɛʎatʃ] |
| | | |
| to shout (vi) | krzyczeć | ['kʃitʃɛtʃ] |
| to show (vt) | pokazywać | [pɔka'zivatʃ] |
| to sign (document) | podpisywać | [pɔtpi'sivatʃ] |
| to sing (vi) | śpiewać | ['ɕpevatʃ] |
| to sit down (vi) | siadać | ['ɕadatʃ] |
| | | |
| to smile (vi) | uśmiechać się | [uɕ'mehatʃ ɕɛ̃] |
| to speak (vi, vt) | rozmawiać | [rɔz'mavʲatʃ] |
| to steal (money, etc.) | kraść | [kraɕtʃ] |
| to stop (please ~ calling me) | przestawać | [pʃɛs'tavatʃ] |
| to study (vt) | studiować | [studʰɔvatʃ] |
| | | |
| to swim (vi) | pływać | ['pwivatʃ] |
| to take (vt) | brać | [bratʃ] |
| to talk to … | rozmawiać | [rɔz'mavʲatʃ] |
| to tell (story, joke) | opowiadać | [ɔpɔ'vʲadatʃ] |
| to thank (vt) | dziękować | [dʒɛ̃'kɔvatʃ] |
| to think (vi, vt) | myśleć | ['miɕletʃ] |
| | | |
| to translate (vt) | tłumaczyć | [twu'matʃitʃ] |
| to trust (vt) | ufać | ['ufatʃ] |
| to try (attempt) | próbować | [pru'bɔvatʃ] |

| | | |
|---|---|---|
| to turn (e.g., ~ left) | **skręcać** | ['skrɛntsatʃ] |
| to turn off | **wyłączać** | [vɨ'wõtʃatʃ] |
| | | |
| to turn on | **włączać** | ['vwõtʃatʃ] |
| to understand (vt) | **rozumieć** | [rɔ'zumetʃ] |
| to wait (vt) | **czekać** | ['tʃɛkatʃ] |
| to want (wish, desire) | **chcieć** | [htʃetʃ] |
| to work (vi) | **pracować** | [pra'tsɔvatʃ] |
| to write (vt) | **pisać** | ['pisatʃ] |

Made in United States
North Haven, CT
29 September 2022

24721458R00063